I Think I Need Marketing

The Knowledge You Need to Build and Manage a Successful Marketing Program

Bonnie Taylor

Dedicated to my mom and husband.
Your support made this book a reality.

Table of Contents

Introduction i

1. Do I Really Need Marketing 1

What Is Marketing? 1
Sales & Marketing Are Not The Same
    Thing 2
Inbound vs. Outbound Marketing 4
    Inbound Marketing 4
    Outbound Marketing 4
    Need To Know: Understanding
        The Marketing World 5

2. I Think I Need A Marketing
    Strategy 7

Identify Your Goals 9
Profile Your Buyers & Marketplace 10
    Need to Know: Buyer &
        Marketplace Profiling 12
Develop Your Brand & Message 13
Evaluate Your Resources 14
Audit Your Current Program 15
Evaluate Your Competition 15
Determine Your Marketing Mix 17
Design Your One To Five Year
    Marketing Plan 18
    Need To Know: How Well Do
        You Know Your Business? 19

3. I Think I Need Branding 21

What Is A Brand and Why Is It

Important? 22
    Corporate Branding 22
    Product Or Service Branding 22
Brand Architecture 23
Developing A Memorable Brand 23
Components Of A Brand Identity 25
    Business Name 26
    Tagline 27
    Logo 29
    Color 31
    Font 31
    Voice & Message 33
    Sound & Smell 33
    Jingles 34
    Packaging 34
    Décor 35
Developing A Style Guide 36
Brand Journey / Brand Experience
    Journey 37
    Brand Journey 37
    Brand Experience Journey 38
Why Re-Brand? 39
Implementing Branding: A Unified
    Effort 40
Protect My Brand 40
    Need To Know: Branding
        Opportunities In Your Business 41

4. I Think I Need A Marketing Mix 45

Developing Your Marketing Mix 41
    Need To Know: Minimal

Marketing 46
Multi-Channel Marketing 46
Content 47
  Need To Know: Creative
    Terminology 48
Advertising 54
  Types of Advertising 54
  Rate Cards & Media Kits 57
  Evaluate the Match 57
  Need To Know: Advertising
    Layout Styles 58
  Placement 59
  Reach 60
  Run 61
  Production Costs 61
  Media Buyers 62
Direct Mail 62
  Print 62
    Bulk Mail 64
  Email 65
    Delivery Methods 66
    CAN-SPAM Act 67
  Frequency 69
  Developing A Mailing List 68
Collateral 69
  Collateral Types 69
Signage 72
Digital Media 74
  Paid Media 74
    Pay Per Click 75
      Google AdWords 75
      Affiliate Programs 77
      Setting a Budget 78
    Search Engine Optimization 78
    Social Media Advertising 80
  Owned Media 81
    Websites 81
      Behind The Scenes 82
      Responsive vs. Mobile 84
      Website Components 85
      Content 86
      User Experience 88
      Landing Pages 90
    Social Media 91
      Allocating Resources 93
      Choosing Your
        Channels 95
      Posting Frequency 98
      Organic vs. Paid Reach 100
    Blogs 101
    Articles 103
    Blog Radio and Podcasts 105

Mobile Apps 106
Videos 108
Webinars 110
Seminars 111
Public Relations 113
  Writing a Press
    Release 113
  Sponsorships 115
Earned Media 116
  Online Reviews 117
    Industry Review Sites 117
    Website & Social Media 118
Trade Shows & Events 119
  Picking The Right Show 120
  Setting Up A Booth Space 121
  Working Your Booth 123
  Trade Show Etiquette 124
Sales Packages / RFI / RFP 125
Need To Know: Design Basics 126

5. I Think I Can Set a Marketing Budget

5. I Think I Can Set a Marketing Budget **127**

Why Do You Need A Budget? 127
Setting Your Marketing Budget 127
Steps To Developing Your Budget 130
Pricing Your Projects 131
Ways to Waste Money In Marketing . 132
  Taking On Too Broad A
    Buying Audience. 133
  Skipping Due Diligence 133
  Nixing Your Marketing Budget ... 133
  Going Overboard On
    Promotional Items 134
  Opting For Cheap Now Leads
    To Spending More In the
    Future 135
  Overruns On Expensive
    Brochures & Sales Folders 136
  Advertising Space &
    Sponsorships 136
  Re-Branding Without Cause 136
  Not Following Up On
    Opportunities 137
  Hosting Open Houses &
    Networking Events 137
  Bundled Projects 138

6. I Think I Can Work With Consultants & Suppliers 139

Articulating Needs.............................139
Read The Contract! 141
Communications 143
Understanding Supplier Roles 143
   Need To Know: Warning Signs
   You've Hired The Wrong Firm.........144
   Marketing Firms 145
      Marketing Strategists...............147
      Branding....................................148
      Communications 149
      Public Relations.......................151
      Researchers...............................152
      Search Engine Optimization /
      Search Engine Management 154
      Social Media.............................155
   Printers..156
      Digital vs. Traditional Press......157
      Sending Files, Packaging............159
      Printing Green..........................161
      Need To Know: Printing Terms 161
   Designers & Creatives....................164
      Working With Designers...........165
      My Project, Not My Files?........166
      Print Design.............................167
      Web Designers & Developers...169
      Photographers &
      Videographers 170
      App, Animator, &
      Game Designers 174
   Writers...177
   Need To Know: Consultant &
   Supplier Titles................................179
Bad Client Actions 182
Radio Silence, Project Killer........182
Withholding Information..............182
Vague Or Off-Topic Responses ...183
Smothering With
   Communication 183
Meeting Deadlines 184
Excessive Meetings.......................184
Excessive Or Vague Revision
   Requests 185

Changing Deadlines Or Terms....187
Asking For Free Work...................187

7. I Think I Need Marketing Research? 189

Research Steps 191
Primary Data 192
   Surveys 192
      Net Promoter Score.................194
   Polls 194
   Focus Groups.................................194
   Interviews.......................................195
   Sample Testing...............................195
   Online Reviews 196
   Observation....................................196
Secondary Data.................................197
Marketing Analytics 198
   Big Data 198
      Big Software Tools...................199
      Customer Relationship
      Management 200
      Enterprise Resource
      Planning...............................201

8. I Think I Can Evaluate My Results 203

Evaluating Results 203
Tracking 205
Leads 207
   Types Of Leads.............................208
   Leads As Indicators......................209
Coupon Codes 210
Response Rates 210
   Clicks...211
Website Visitor Tracking..................212

9. I Think I Can Handle Success . 213

Acknowledgements................. 217

Bibliography 219

About the Author 221

Introduction

"What kind of pens do you sell?"

That simple question, asked to me by a third person in a month's time, was the turning point leading up to this book. Writing a book about marketing has been on my mind for years, but other projects always took precedent and "my book" was pushed further down my list. It finally took a question about pens by well-meaning but woefully out of touch business owners to make this book my priority.

You may be wondering what's the big deal why would pens lead to a marketing book? I'll agree that on the surface a question about pens is innocent enough, but as a follow-up question to my stating, "I'm a marketer," it was telling and, ultimately, highly motivational.

I've been a marketing professional for over twenty years and have worked with clients in countless industries, marketing business to business and business to consumer, both products and services, domestically and internationally, and have found marketing to be one of the most universally misunderstood and misapplied business roles. That's not to say every business struggles with marketing. Clearly, some are knocking it out of the park and growing by leaps and bounds; however, too many experienced professionals I meet can readily define "accounting" or list ways a lawyer can benefit a business, but then stumble when asked to define "marketing."

Meeting smart business people who don't thoroughly grasp marketing is hardly an unusual experience. It's a tough field to break down, and unless one has worked in marketing for some time, it's anything but intuitive. This is a shame because few business areas can make or break a business as quickly and effectively as marketing.

Is understanding marketing really that big of a deal in business? Yes, and I propose that it's much more than a big deal; it's actually vital, because no business can survive without the customers or income marketing provides. None. It's just not possible. I suppose a business can exist on life support with an infusion from an owner's life savings or other funding source, but even that can't ultimately save a business lacking customers.

When I look at the high numbers of businesses that fail each year and consider the role marketing should play within a business, it's easy for me to see some sort of connection between the two, which is why my pens question ultimately matters a great deal.

Anyone who has sat in meetings or board rooms and sweated over profit and loss, work forecasts, expansion plans, and quarter over quarter change reports and realized business isn't moving forward as projected, has thought, I think (hope) marketing can fix this.

That's why this book exists. To clear up any confusion on when, how, and what kind of marketing works in various business situations and how to properly use it to your advantage. It covers how to hire the right person and not be gouged or sold projects you don't need simply because you don't understand.

It's my hope that this book will help you, my reader, and business owners and managers everywhere gain a better understanding of marketing's true role and how you can embrace it as a path toward future growth. My goal is share my experience and knowledge to clear up any confusion surrounding marketing and provide you with the tools you need to successfully set up and manage your own business's marketing department.

I wish you success in your future marketing efforts!

- Bonnie Taylor

1. Do I Really Need Marketing

What Is Marketing?

Before I address the question of whether or not you need marketing, let me first ask you a few questions:

1. Are you in business?

2. If so, does your business require money to support staff, pay bills, and purchase business infrastructure?

3. Does this money come from customers, clients, or donors (known henceforth as "buyers")?

If you answered 'yes' to any of these questions, your business's survival depends on successfully attracting and engaging potential buyers. Why? Simply put, marketing is an investment in your future buyers. It's the process of planning and executing mass messaging with an intent to motivate and engage potential buyers. It's about creating customer experiences that ultimately lead to product or service buy-in and trust. It's through marketing that your business communicates its message to your buyer and helps them achieve brand awareness.

This mass messaging can take many forms and styles across numerous platforms: it can be bold or subtle, traditional or cutting edge, trend setting or timely, publicly displayed or delivered directly to your buyers' homes.

No matter what tools your marketing program employs, its ultimate goal is keeping your business in front of your targeted buying audience's eyes,

If you think about your own recent purchases you'll understand how marketing can influence buyers. Did you make your purchase randomly and without consideration or did you spend time researching and considering different brands? Why did you purchase from a particular store or web site? Did you pick up your purchases and review packaging before checking out? Were you influenced by media attention and public excitement? If you were an early iPhone adopter, you've experienced marketing's ability to generate excitement and purchasing frenzy first-hand. Yes, marketing's that powerful.

When properly executed, marketing yields its colossal power wisely, turning naysayers into advocates, shooting your business to the top of your industry, and guiding future buyers to your doorstep. It's through research and proper planning that your marketing program becomes the path toward your business's future growth.

With so much business potential, it's no surprise that the marketing world is a confusing place strewn with muddied terminology and grandiose promises. When we evaluate it by the various business approaches, distinguishing between business to business (B2B), business to consumer (B2C), product marketing, and service marketing, it becomes that much more complicated.

Sales & Marketing Are Not the Same Thing

One of the first steps in clearing up marketing's confusion involves appreciating the difference between marketing and sales. You may have been thinking why do I need marketing if I have a sales team? Let me clear that misconception up first.

Sales and marketing are not interchangeable. True, they both target buyers in an effort to bring in business; however, expecting your sales team to manage marketing activities or your marketer to handle sales calls waters down both efforts and is a misuse of your teams' skill sets. Each role requires a specialized approach, and asking for crossover could lead to staff frustration, poor messaging, and burnout. Success in each requires a focused effort and constant attention.

The reality is that sales and marketing are unique roles. While they complement each other, each approaches buyers differently. Sales is a two-way conversation. It's a chance to speak one on one with a potential buyer and immediately address individual concerns (i.e., barriers to sales), and customize a pitch on the fly. Marketing, on the other hand, is designed for the masses. It's typically remotely executed, and, while customization does factor in, it's with a targeted buying audience, not an individual buyer, in mind.

Confusion in a sales vs. marketing debate is understandable as sales situations can and should be a by-product of a successful marketing program. Through carefully crafted and targeted messaging, buyers are "warmed up" by marketing, helping sales in its efforts. Completely cold calls can turn into new buyers, of course, but the amount of sales work involved is exponentially increased if a buyer has never heard of your business before.

Ideally, sales and marketing work side by side toward common goals, with each respecting the other's methods and processes. It's nearly impossible to achieve real and sustainable growth without both efforts. Marketing can directly generate sales situations, such as phone calls or website requests following a buyer's viewing of your advertisement or online video, and many sales teams rely on marketing created materials during presentations. Sales can deliver invaluable feedback on how a business's products or services have been received by the marketplace, including data on marketplace trends, buyer-specific information, and responses to your brand and marketing program itself.

Inbound vs. Outbound Marketing

There are many ways to classify marketing efforts. The simplest breaks efforts into two approaches: inbound marketing and outbound marketing. Most modern marketing programs employ a mix of the two. Your own marketplace and internal resources will dictate the weight you assign to each approach.

Inbound Marketing

Given the volume of marketing messages competing for your buyers' attention each day, it's no surprise that information they seek out themselves has a powerful marketing advantage. Known as **inbound marketing**, this approach refers to information created by your business to draw buyers into your brand. Rather than screaming "buy our product," inbound marketing activities strive for quality and topical sharing that buyers find helpful, informative, and / or entertaining. How-to videos, articles, blog posts, and social media are examples of inbound marketing. It's a softer approach that is an exchange of information for your buyers' time.

Inbound marketing allows buyers to freely engage with your brand in a relatively "sales-free" setting. The quality of information offered, coupled with ease of use, can encourage longer and repeat buyer-brand interactions, resulting in a form of brand loyalty.

With an emphasis on solving buyers' needs, inbound marketing strengthens an impression of expertise while exploring your business's own depth of service or product offering. Moreover, inbound marketing has a secondary goal of encouraging the sharing and dissemination of your business's message by buyers to other potential buyers.

Outbound Marketing

Conversely, **outbound marketing** activities are straight-forward requests for a purchase or buyer action. Rather than relying on a buyer to be drawn

Outbound marketing is obvious in its messaging and spurs immediate action.

into your brand, outbound marketing seeks buyers and addresses them directly. Outbound marketing will unashamedly promote your business, tout its unique identifiers, and directly request buy-in. A call to action is obviously displayed, resulting in, however skillfully applied, a more "in-your-face" marketing style.

Outbound marketing can't be mistaken for anything other than a marketing effort. There's often a sense of urgency in outbound marketing and, when properly executed, it can be highly effective, leading to immediate results. Messaging through this approach is used to promote sales, events, new services or products, etc. Advertisements, direct mail, collateral, and trade shows are all examples of outbound marketing.

Need To Know: Understanding The Marketing World

Marketing Strategy: Your business's master marketing plan. It includes market research, buyer profiles, competitive reviews, branding and program audits, campaign concepts, opportunities, and an activity calendar into one document. It is your business's overreaching brain trust under which all other marketing falls. Other efforts or departments should work together toward achieving milestones and goals set forth in your marketing strategy.

Branding: Includes all activities that convey your business's outward facing image and internal business personality, combined. Your branding will dictate everything from your logo to the communication style (or voice) used in your marketing to the music played in your retail store.

Marketing Communications: Marketing communications (often abbreviated "MarCom") is a global term applied to all forms of marketing messaging between a business and buyer. It includes content, direct mail, websites, collateral, social media, etc. MarCom can be subdivided into type, as with print or digital communications. Depending on the depth and structure of your business's marketing program, you may include or segment out floating efforts like advertising and Search Engine Optimization / Search Engine Management (SEO / SEM).

Research / Analytics: Marketing is far less effective without knowledge on your business's buyers, marketplace, and competitors. Market research includes a wide variety of data-gathering efforts ranging from demographic data research to more business specific information garnered through surveys and visitor tracking. Analytics is the interpretation and compilation of these results.

Events: A rare in-person activity within the marketing world, events includes any planned business appearance targeting a mass audience. Trade shows, business-managed seminars, and open house events are all events.

Public Relations: Although untrue when one calculates the amount of time and effort involved, public relations (often abbreviated "PR") is frequently referred to as "free advertising" because it involves unpaid placement or mentions within the media. PR commonly begins with a press releases sent to journalists or media outlets, who may choose to report your information as news. Sponsorships are another form of PR because they're usually a sense of goodwill and supportive effort rather than high-return marketing.

2. I Think I Need A Marketing Strategy

Considering all the options available within marketing, it may be difficult to choose a starting point. Without a doubt, the best investment you'll make in your business is a **marketing strategy**. Why? Because having one provides you with an educated action plan for reaching and enticing your targeted buyers. I've established that your business can't survive without buyers; therefore, strategically mapping out your marketing steps is an exercise toward reaching buyers and achieving business growth. Trying to find your buyers without a critical review of your business and carefully planned action steps based on solid intelligence is nearly impossible. If you can envision a person walking down a business path, casually tossing money in all directions without a glance as to where and to whom her money might reach, you'll instantly grasp what business is like without a marketing strategy; paying to blindly throw your message at your buyers, hoping and praying they'll make a purchase.

In short, marketing strategies exist and are singularly created with business growth in mind. Unlike a business plan that covers operations, management, systems, processes, and your overall business structure, your marketing strategy is singularly focused on the tools and activities that enhance or detract from your business's ability to reach its growth goals. Your business plan may touch on marketing, but its approach and information are nothing like what you'll find in a strategy.

Marketing strategies not only deliver a high ROI, but also ease business pain by putting your entire program on a clear and purposeful track. While I've written many strategies over the years, the positive impact they have on a business never fails to make me smile. I fondly remember one client who had struggled for over ten years to gain a foothold with his health product, whose business went from selling a few products a month domestically to hundreds of thousands a week internationally after implementing my strategy. It's a great feeling!

How is this possible? A marketing strategy not only addresses current challenges and maps out paths by which your business can grow in the future, it also audits your business's brand and message, ensuring that the two sync up your products or services with your targeted buyers and marketplace. It's a combination of big picture and detail analysis that incorporates a wide range of marketing channels tailored for your unique industry, market, resources, and budget. In other words, it's an entirely custom document that has but one goal in mind: your business's growth.

A word of caution, however, about creating your marketing strategy. A professionally crafted marketing strategy is an investment in saving money because it targets your marketing efforts and helps avoid waste. A poorly crafted strategy, on the other hand, has a negative business effect because they often skip vital steps and push ill advised efforts. Tragically, marketing strategies are often put aside to gather dust or, worse yet, the effort is skipped altogether by smaller business as a cost savings decision or through a lack of appreciation for their worth.

While there are basic questions that kick off the strategic process, for a marketing strategy to be truly effective, it needs to be a customized effort involving research, analysis, and a careful matching of opportunities with the business's resources and budget. This can never be a quick or off the shelf effort. An effective marketing strategy takes time and expertise to develop properly.

Expertise is critical to the marketing strategy process. Crafting a master plan that's both successful and budget-conscious is a skill acquired through experience and specific marketing training, not something sketched out by a rep at a service shop or from a generic, "small business strategy" check list. There are no shortcuts in writing your strategy!

An effective marketing strategy will present a mix of opportunities that meet your immediate goals and demonstrate paths for growth (it will never force your business beyond its means). The result is a clear audit of your business in its current state, a review of who you are targeting as a buyer, an evaluation of your marketing budget, and an intelligently developed plan and schedule for reaching your buyers.

Identify Your Goals

The best map in the world is an utterly useless navigation tool without an identified destination. So it is with a marketing strategy. Before you can implement any marketing, you first need to identify your short and long term business goals. Be specific and be truthful with yourself. Questions you'll need to address, include:

- What is my business's ultimate goal?

- Am I comfortable with my business's current market or would I like it to change?

- What services or products would I like to add to my business?

- What growth goals do I realistically think my business can achieve in six months? One year? Five years? Are these tied to employees, geography, revenue, or all three?

- What services or products do I think will help my business achieve these goals?

Answering these and similar questions will help you hone in on your goals, both realistic and wished. Vague responses like "world domination" will do little to help you realize your business goals, whereas answers such as "open three additional offices in cities A, B, and C" will. Don't discount your dream goals! Evaluating any differences between your realistic and wished for goals can be helpful to your goal setting process.

Profile Your Buyers & Marketplace

Every decision you make in marketing should directly link with your buyer and marketplace. It simply isn't possible to run a successful marketing program without fully understanding the buyers upon which your livelihood depends. Your business can't and shouldn't try marketing to the world; therefore, you need to narrow down and target a buying group. As a marketer, it baffles me how any business can open its doors without taking the time to first evaluate to whom it will sell its services and products and from whom it will grab market share.

Questions such as, "how many buyers are out there?", "how do they like to be reached?", and, "who am I competing against?" are all fundamental to business success because it's only through this knowledge that a business can adapt and grow. Known as **buyer and marketplace profiles**, this invaluable data creates a target that will drive everything from your branding to campaign themes to package design. Profiles should be created for each new market you wish to enter before you spend a single campaign dollar. This will ensure your business is culturally respectful and aligned with any new markets (not using breezy California girl bikini billboards in Saudi Arabia, for example).

The first step in profiling is to pull information from your own historic buyer interactions. Established businesses have an obvious advantage over startups at this stage as they can pull purchase patterns, website and social media traffic, and inquiry data. By evaluating who has traditionally responded to your brand and correlating that information with your sales and profitability reports, you'll have a **historic buyer profile**.

The second step is to look at your marketplace itself. Identify your current geographic reach and match that up with your goals. Are you local and

Targeting buyers will help you save money and focus your marketing efforts.

looking to expand? Do you have multiple locations, some faring better than others? Dig into the demographics of the marketplace and evaluate who lives and shops within its borders. Don't forget to look at the market itself. Are there physical concerns such as traffic congestion or scheduled road work that could impact your business? Are you priced above the typical buyer's income? If you have a retail location, is it in a highly visible and easily accessed location?

This step takes time and isn't entertaining, but skipping it could be detrimental to future business growth. Information on the population living and shopping within your targeted market can include income, age range, education level, shopping habits, traffic flow, voting patterns, and much more. Growth, business density, rent prices, and occupancy rates will show the viability and receptiveness of the market. A visual evaluation will give you an impression of the market's health. Are your target buyers walking around with shopping bags or working in the area? Is the area litter and graffiti free? Are signs and building facades fresh or dated?

Be critical in this step. This is an excellent time to ask if it's really a viable and sustainable market for your business. Remember, the market has to be a fit with your business's unique brand and product or service offerings. For example, if rent prices in the area are high, your products' profit margins low, and buyer density numbers light, that market isn't a good fit. It's easy to fail with the right product or service in the wrong market.

The third step is to create a **competitive profile**. Will you face competition in the targeted market? If yes, how much is acceptable? In what ways are these businesses competition? Is your competition targeting the same type of buyer as your business? Why or why not? Whenever possible, secret shop the competition and compare their rates, products or services, and locations with your own. Evaluate how the competition has been successful and where have they fallen short.

At this point switch perspectives and evaluate the marketplace from your buyer profile's point of view, again shopping the competition. Look at the business's geographic reach and investigate both demographic data and local economic growth plans. All of this data will play into the final evaluation of whether you should continue in your current market or branch out into an area that's buyer-rich.

Need To Know: Buyer And Marketplace Profiling

Buyer and marketplace profiles hold a valuable place within your marketing program. With this knowledge, you can predict and modify your efforts to yield the greatest result:

- **Historic Buyer Profile:** What type of buyer has supported your business in the past? Break that buyer type into demographic and purchasing data.

- **Marketplace Data:** Profile who is shopping in the market using demographic data. Review the marketplace as a whole and ask what does the market look like, economically and physically?

- **Competitive Profile:** Will you face competition in this market? How are they faring in the market? Why?

Develop Your Brand & Message

Once you've identified your business goals and truly understand your marketplace, it's time to critically review and / or develop your business's **brand**.

A brand is your business's public look and message. It's the embodiment of your culture and business vision. It embraces your goals and charges forward to meet them head on. Brand is both an identifier and differentiator, allowing you to bring your message to life through **branding**. I'll expand on brands and branding in Chapter 3, but for right now, know that your marketing strategy will audit and address any weaknesses within your brand.

Businesses all have the beginning of a brand–an official name recorded when the entity was formed. Some have taken steps to identify a logo, tagline, and possibly a general color scheme or style guide. Your marketing strategy needs to thoroughly evaluate your brand, starting with your business name, before moving on to other aspects of your business. Keep in mind that branding is not an opportunity to showcase your personal taste or personal impressions. To be successful, your brand has to match up with your buyers.

This stage of your marketing strategy is referred to as a **brand audit** as it will thoroughly evaluate your brand through expert and unbiased eyes. An experienced marketing strategist will actually conduct two audits, one as a buyer and another as a marketer. Knowing that your brand's mission is to quickly convey your business's vision and story, the brand audit will need to dig into whether or not your brand targets your appropriate buyer and is in keeping with her buyer habits. Is it unique enough within the marketplace to set your business apart from your competition? With established brands, the marketing strategy will highlight any brand challenges, inconsistencies, or weaknesses before suggesting modifications and improvements.

Unfortunately, brand seems to be a point at which many smaller businesses abandon their strategic efforts. Your business's brand is essential and well worth a hefty effort, but branding alone isn't enough of an action item to grow your business and isn't where your marketing should end.

Evaluate Your Resources

Resources are a key component of any marketing strategy. After all, it's easy to spend a fortune based on an ideal, but if your business can't support that level of spending, the strategy will fail. Not every business can devote millions of dollars and a full team of experienced staff members to its marketing efforts. Therefore, your business's unique resources must factor into your marketing strategy. Resources can be calculated by:

Resources = Budget + Staff Expertise + Time Available

I'll cover marketing budgets more thoroughly in Chapter 5, but suffice it to say, building a strategy with high-priced marketing projects won't work if your budget is in the four digits. The goal is not to put your business into debt! Each step and current / planned / possible project must factor in with what your business can reasonably handle.

Staff expertise and the time that can be allotted to marketing efforts is of tremendous importance when working through your marketing strategy. If your team consists of junior employees or professionals of a different skill set, your marketing strategy should take into account training, time lost to a learning curve, and your having to outsource work. Additionally, the amount of time your team has available has to factor into your program. If, for example, you or your team can realistically dedicate only a few hours each week, then signing up for five or six social media accounts isn't a sustainable plan.

Many businesses have low cost and free marketing options already at their disposal and may not realize it. A good marketing strategy created by an experienced expert will review your business's internal options, evaluate the business as a whole, and discover resources that can be used in your marketing plan. I like to empower my clients in my strategies by giving them the chance to save their budget for bigger ticket items down the road.

Audit Your Current Program

Your marketing should never be static or trapped in a single period's evaluation. Which is why auditing your current marketing program is not only the next step in a marketing strategy, but also a smart ongoing practice. **Marketing audits** extend beyond branding to review all of your business's marketing efforts, deconstructing your program to determine weaknesses and strengths. It's at this stage that wasted money or time are discovered, schedules and timing broken down, and missed opportunities highlighted. Occasionally an audit will discover a project that started down a positive path in the past, but was either abandoned too early or its message wasn't quite right.

Your marketing program audit will seek out strengths as well as holes and weaknesses by dissecting the marketing channel mix, frequency, and more, then match and compare the entire program with your targeted buyer and market profiles. Particular care should be spent on larger marketing efforts such as your website, brochures, newsletters, social media, and retail branding, if applicable. The program should also be evaluated in terms of staff resources, factoring any strengths into the final evaluation.

Audits aren't a time for indulging emotional connections or wearing blinders. You'll have to be realistic, all-encompassing, and unflinchingly honest for your work to have a positive effective. If you feel you are too close to your business to disengage emotionally, you'll need to bring in a neutral expert who can be critically honest.

Evaluate Your Competition

"Who is my competition and how do we differ?" That's a question you should be able to answer at any given time! The next step in your marketing strategy is to thoroughly evaluate your business's competition. More than by name alone, you should be aware of who is snagging market share from you and how each competitor compares with your business in products or services, quality, customer service, messaging, and overall marketing efforts. Yours may have the best product or be the best service

Toyota and Subway used the *Muppets Most Wanted* movie launch--and its stars--as part of their respective marketing programs.

provider available, but that won't mean anything if the competition is signing more buyers!

Your market research should have identified any competition in each targeted marketplace. In this stage of your marketing strategy, you should take that information, evaluate and rank each in terms of market share, product or service offerings (identifying which are directly competing with your own), promotions, location, price, and branding. As much as possible, you should compare each competitor's marketing program against your own.

Competitive profiles should also include a form of secret shopping using an unbiased buyer's approach, be it business to business or business to consumer. I like to analyze competitors for ways their products or services could satisfy my buyer needs, entice me to make a purchase, or turn me off as a buyer.

You may want to create a table listing each competitor's attributes to make comparisons easier. Keep this information up to date, adding promotions or news items as they surface. Make a practice of checking in on your competition on a regular schedule, either monthly or quarterly.

Determine Your Marketing Mix

This stage of a marketing strategy is really a game of, 'attracting buyers.' This is the most strategic stage of your strategy, but one that couldn't exist without all the previous steps. I'll go into more depth on determining your marketing mix in Chapter 4, but it's at this point that your strategy should answer questions such as, "should my business adopt the latest trends or stick to more traditional methods?", "can I achieve growth using my current resources or should I outsource?" or "what will provide the biggest bang for a limited budget?"

Example Marketing Calendar

| | January | | | | | February | | | | |
	Week 1	Week 2	Week 3	Week 4	Week 5	Week 1	Week 2	Week 3	Week 4	Week 5
Advertising										
Print	Campaign 1: Post and Times full pages Jan 8, 15, 22, 30							Campaign 2		
Digital		Campaign 1: Digital post, 20,000 impressions Jan 22 - Feb 3							Campaign 2: Digital post, 20,000 impressions Feb 17 - March 10	
PPC	Campaign 1					Campaign 2				
Radio		Campaign 1: 24 :30 spots			Campaign 1: 24 :30 spots		Campaign 2: 24 :30 spots			Campaign 2: 24 :30 spots
Direct Mail										
Post card	Campaign 1: Drop 1			Campaign 1: Drop 2		Campaign 2: Drop 1			Campaign 2: Drop 2	
Email		Campaign 1: Drop 1		Campaign 1: Drop 2			Campaign 1: Drop 1		Campaign 1: Drop 2	
Newsletter		Campaign 1: Drop 1					Campaign 2: Drop 1			
Events										
Trade Shows	Show 1: Vegas Industry show Jan 6			Show 2: New Orleans Expo, Jan 24				Show 3: Chicago ULW Annual: Feb 18		
Online										
Web Site	Launch new pages					Launch new pages				
Blog	Topic 1	Topic 2	Topic 3	Topic 4	Topic 5	Topic 6	Topic 7	Topic 8	Topic 9	Topic 10
Twitter	Campaign 1 Push			Campaign 1 Push		Campaign 2 Push			Campaign 2 Push	
Facebook	Campaign 1 Push					Campaign 2 Push				
LinkedIn	Campaign 1 Push					Campaign 2 Push				
Public Relations										
Press Releases	Campaign 1 Drop					Campaign 2 Drop				

Tracking your efforts on a marketing calendar will help you maintain campaign details, prevent overlaps, and meet deadlines.

It's also the stage where experience really pays off as there are many, many ways to spend (and waste) money in marketing and only so many options that will reach your right buyers. I enjoy this stage the most and spend time looking under rocks to discover new options and find cost effective solutions. Due to unique attributes within businesses themselves, no two strategies should ever be the same at this stage, making this the most custom portion of the entire process.

This is also the most flexible portion of your marketing strategy and should include a variety of options that range from 'incorporate immediately' to more longer term efforts that make sense once the business has grown or has put other marketing tools in place. A good mix will utilize multiple marketing channels and allow a business to reach buyers on many levels.

Design Your One To Five Year Marketing Plan

Every marketing strategy should wrap up with an action plan. The minimum breakdown should be a one year marketing calendar broken out by month, with longer reaching efforts on a two to five year plan. Your marketing plan should list carefully selected marketing efforts determined in the strategy and provide a schedule for when they should be launched and evaluated. Holidays, peak business seasons, product or service launches, special events, etc. should all be incorporated into this calendar.

For smaller businesses or those working on a limited budget, I try to stick with lower cost efforts that can be maintained internally while the business grows. Optional efforts that may cost more money can be pushed until after an early goal has been achieved. More expensive or involved opportunities are generally reserved for a two to five year plan and are contingent upon achieving goals.

Need To Know: How Well Do You Know Your Business?

The following are questions you should be able to answer quickly and succinctly. Your data should be kept up to date, reflecting market and business changes:

- Why are you in business?

- What are your realistic business goals, today, six months, one year, or five years from today? What's on your wish list?

- Who are your buyers? Accurately profile a buyer type for each product or service.

- What is your geographic reach? In other words, *where* is your marketplace?

- Do your different products or services fare better within different markets or with various buyers?

- Who are your competitors? Are you tracking their activities?

- How is your business perceived within the marketplace? How do you know this (surveys, comments, direct feedback)?

- How is your business? Is it on a rise? Have you hit a plateau? Are sales declining?

- Which are your best-selling products or services? Which are your worst? Where are they within their life cycles?

- What resources can you realistically devote to marketing? Is this sustainable?

3. I Think I Need Branding

Misunderstanding surrounds the marketing term, **branding**. What I've found is that while most business owners know they need branding, many don't understand how it should be used or the effort required to develop and maintain a memorable brand. Consequently their best intentioned branding efforts fall flat and fail to deliver.

It's important to understand that while developing a memorable brand is important to your business's success, it's only one of many components in a successful marketing program. Branding is not an either / or with the rest of your marketing program, but rather a sub-segment of marketing that should be created through careful research and planning, in accordance with the information discovered in a marketing strategy. Branding is the window dressing that will dictate the image your business presents to the world. It isn't your entire program.

Branding can't act alone because "brand" is neither a process nor an activity by which a business interacts with buyers. It embodies your business vision, but is not a vehicle for telling your complete story. Branding won't overcome a poor marketing communications program (how will buyers know about your brand without communication?), develop a campaign, combat outdated technology such as in websites, or address all barriers to purchase.

Given the above, why should you invest time and money into developing and maintaining your brand?

What Is A Brand And Why Is It Important?

A **brand** is your business's unique, intentional, and easily recognized identifier. It's the overall impression a buyer has of your business, drawn from marketing sources, first-hand experiences, and reputation. Good or bad, your brand evokes emotion, spurs a reaction, and incites an opinion.

Your brand should help a buyer develop a personal connection and loyalty with your business. It should generate interest in your products and services, and start buyers on the path toward making a purchase. Your brand will manifest itself obviously in your logo, tagline message, color scheme, and design style, and less obviously in areas like your communications voice, buyer approach, and décor.

Creating a marketing program by which your brand is consistently presented to a buying audience is called branding. In simplest terms, branding is the set of rules that dictates items such as the colors used in design, the tense and style in communication, types of supportive graphics and photos, the décor of an office or retail store, and the placement of a logo. In the creative world, these rules are also known as **style guides** and should be referred to in all marketing activities.

Corporate Branding

Corporate Branding refers to a corporate identifier where a business name is the brand's focus. All services or products are grouped under a single brand. Corporate branding is ideal for single line businesses lacking subsidiaries or business verticals, and, for many businesses, this type of branding is all that's needed to achieve market awareness. Not restricted to corporations, it can be adopted by any business, nonprofit, individual, educational entity, etc. where the name of the business is the brand.

Product Or Service Branding

There are times when it makes sense to develop brands within a core brand that are specifically focused on a product(s) or service(s). You would employ this type of branding to distinguish a product or service apart from your core business, allowing for a more focused marketing effort. In this situation, your marketing's targeted goal is to create brand loyalty with an individual product or service, not necessarily with your business itself. An example of this is the brand *Band-Aid*, which is a product line marketed by its parent business, Johnson & Johnson.

Brand Architecture

The use of vertical and subsidiary businesses can necessitate your business presenting slightly different branding faces to different buyers or markets. Known as **brand architecture**, the structure is designed to show a main, or parent brand, as the primary business face shown at the top of a hierarchy. Business verticals or subsidiaries are then marketed as unique brands under the parent brand, using slight modification to represent their different service or product lines, business names, etc. Your business and market will influence how these subsidiary brands are different, but typically brand architecture is accomplished through color with corresponding name changes or through variations of a tagline or logo.

Developing A Memorable Brand

How will you develop a brand that inspires loyalty, evokes emotion, creates a claim, and uniquely identifies your business? It starts with the research data gathered while creating your business's marketing strategy. More specifically, your will need any information gathered about your targeted buying audience and marketplace plus your business's profile, goals, history, and competition. All of this information feeds the brand development process:

Position. The first step in developing your brand is to evaluate your business's culture, value, products or services, and personality. Questions to ask yourself at this stage include:

- Is your business serious or playful?

- Local or worldwide?

- Service-oriented or strictly product?

- Environmentally conscious?

- Targeting other businesses (B2B) or public consumers (B2C)?

A well-developed brand takes all of this into account and reflects your business's position through message, color, marketing style, and experience. I once had a new client who wanted to convey a sense of strength, power,

Brand Architecture At Work

Brand architecture unifies all business verticals and subsidiaries under a core brand while allowing each to have a unique identity.

Amazon.com, Inc.'s parent company sets the look and overall brand style:

amazon.com

Amazon.com, Inc.'s many business verticals incorporate elements of its parent company brand, but have their own brand identities. Examples include:

amazonkindle

amazon.com Prime

amazon.com Smile
You shop. **Amazon gives.**

amazon instant video

amazon game studios

amazon web services

and dependability through his brand, yet he used a weak, thinly outlined logo and generic language. His current brand's style was a complete mismatch with what he desired in his business's self-image.

Business claim. The next step is to resolve your business's claim, also known as your value proposition. Your brand should give targeted buyers an understanding of why your business exists and how its products or services will resolve their needs and wants better than your competition's products or services. This is called the business's claim, which is calculated by:

Business Claim = Why Your Business Exists + Your Competition + Your Targeted Buyer and Market Profile

Credibility. Your brand should quickly convey a sense of business credibility, which is why this is the next step in the brand development process. Logos, color scheme, packaging, social media, websites, chosen imagery, etc. all will impact your brand's credibility by working as subliminal buyer influencers. For example, color could instantly evoke either a trustworthy or heated emotional response in your buyer, depending on your choice. In-person encounters with a brand's credibility are found in location, décor, types of services or products offered (especially true in retail), and customer service and cleanliness.

Target an audience. The last step in developing a brand is to evaluate your buyers, keeping trends in mind. By using the research conducted for your marketing strategy, you'll have a buyer profile in hand, including an understanding of their likes and dislikes. Your brand should take these buyer preferences into account and "speak" directly to your buyer.

Components Of A Brand Identity

While "branding" includes a unified, business-wide effort, your **brand identity** itself can be broken out into a few different components, all important contributors to a successful brand effort. It's important not to get bogged down at this stage. You may throw out a few ideas early on, especially when working on your business's name. Don't become frustrated; it takes time to develop a meaningful brand! I like to tackle each component of a brand identity one at a time, looking for ways they all mesh and feed into each other to create the perfect brand.

Business Name

The first element of any brand is a business name. The name must be memorable, understandable, and stand for something. No pressure! It's the hardest working component in your brand's identity, and will make its way into every nook and cranny within your business. Your name has to be right.

Naming a business can be an exhausting process! Finding a single word or set of words that completely embraces your business's values, services or products, and culture is no small feat and can take time. Be prepared to go through many ideas before settling on the right one. Remember, this is not a time for egos or sentimentality. Your business's name will be used in every conceivable business situation, well beyond marketing's borders, making research and marketplace evaluation more important than owner emotions.

There's a mistaken notion held by some that a name must directly describe a business's products or services for it to be successful. No offense to "Al's Plumbing and Seasonal Flower Shop," but Google and Amazon.com, Inc. have managed just fine without a descriptive name! It's important to note that business names using made up words or obscure references may require more up-front branding just to help buyers understand who and what you are; however, the effort can be well worth it when the result is a unique and memorable name.

Locational Names. As a rule, locational names can be limiting and often create a branding challenge later in the business's life cycle. If, for example, your business name includes your town, buyers may see your business as too small because, as the name suggests, it's locked by a single geographic location. Locational names can become a serious hindrance if your business moves or expands in the future. At best the name may confuse buyers as to where you're really located and, at worst, your new buyers may not warm up to a business named after a different location. It's best to avoid the headache and drop the location in your name.

Proper Names. As tempting and rewarding as it may be to name your business after yourself, it's not always a wise decision. Using your initials, last name, or possessively claiming your business (remember Al's?) can all scream "small" in buyers' minds. It may also impact interest if your goal is to sell your business in the future or cause a major re-branding effort if one member of a multi-named business leaves. There are exceptions to this rule—Marie Calendar and her famous pies comes to mind—and some business types like legal practices where using names is commonplace. Generally speaking, however, names will limit your business's size in buyers' minds, especially early in your life cycle.

Legality. Once you settle on a name you like, it's important to check that it hasn't already been taken before you order business cards. Your research should include multiple checks at both the state and national level. Good first steps include your State Corporate Commission and the U.S. Small Business Administration. Both have search pages that will allow you to check previously registered and active entities. If it's free and clear, register as a new business entity and set about creating the next components of your brand.

Tagline

Summing up your business in a few words is a tough task, particularly when the chosen words have the additional responsibility of differentiating your business from the competition while simultaneously drawing potential buyers into your brand. Also known as a business slogan or catchphrase, a well crafted **tagline** takes on this challenge and can become as, if not more, recognizable than your brand's other elements (Milk Processor

Education Program's "Got Milk?" and Nike, Inc.'s "Just do it" taglines are good examples).

The best taglines share similar traits. They're typically short, punchy, and easy to remember. They differentiate their business from the competition while emphasizing a competitive advantage. They elicit an emotional response from buyers. They're also positive representatives of their brands and achieve their creative goal of generating interest.

Your business may use one tagline throughout your business's lifetime or have several for use in different markets or attached to different services or products. It's not unusual for a single business to slightly vary its tagline when addressing different buyers.

Taglines By Type

Taglines are typically categorized by the type of action or wished for emotional response. These categories are:

Specific. Specific taglines tell buyers about the business's products or services, as in CNN's,

> *"The most trusted name in news."*

Imperative. Imperative taglines spur a buyer action, as in YouTube's,

> *"Broadcast yourself."*

Provocative. Provocative taglines form a question that will make buyers stop and ponder, such as in The Wendy Company's famous,

> *"Where's the beef?"*

Descriptive. Descriptive taglines talk about their businesses' products or services, such as Target Corporation's,

> *"Expect more, Pay less."*

Superlative. Created to promote a business as the best, Superlative taglines set their brands at the top of the pedestal, such as Budweiser's,

> *"The king of beers."*

Logo

The graphic identity of your brand, your **logo**, can be comprised of your business's name, graphics, or a combination of the two. Your logo should not only realize your business's vision, but also quickly and simply convey its culture and message. The need to be both unique and enticing makes logo design one of the trickier branding steps.

Logos, also know as "brand marks," "trademarks," and "brand symbols", can find life through a variety of styles. As long as you're not infringing on another's trademarked design, your options are limitless.

Marketing research and devices used to develop the business's name should be employed throughout your logo design process. Your logo will be a heavy lifter in your branding program and needs to hit upon the same market influencers identified earlier. If you think about it, your logo will be used throughout your business, from signage to invoices, and act as the visual reference buyers use when thinking of your brand. It has to stand out. It has to be right.

Beware, logo design is an area where smaller businesses fall victim to discount design outlets or inexperienced graphic designers who don't fully realize a brand's mission. The logo development process is not as much about design as it is "branding." Quite a bit of thought and research should go into your logo's construction, which simply isn't going to happen at the discount level. Discount logo providers may invest time in creating a design with the intent of recouping their effort by selling the design to many businesses at a lower price. If you purchase one of these logos, it's quite possible you may see it again attached to another business's name.

Variations Within Logo Styles

Business Name. Logos can be structured using nothing more than your business's name as a design element: The Coca-Cola Company, eBay Inc.

Letterform. Logo design that uses letters as mnemonic symbols of the business's name: International Business Machines Corporation, Unilever

Emblems. Logo design that embeds a business name within a design element: MasterCard Incorporated, IKEA

Pictorial. Logo design centered around a recognizable, yet stylized image: Apple Inc., Starbucks Coffee Company

Symbol. Logo designed around an abstract, created image: Nike, Inc., McDonalds Corporation

Color

Your industry and type of business can influence your **color** choices. Why? Because buyers interpret and react to colors, applying different emotions to each. Choosing a color is an exercise in subliminal influence, as your choice of color or color combinations can have a psychological impact on your buyers. You may decide to pick a Pantone® Matching System (PMS) color already listed in one of the company's color guides or have your own custom mixed. Businesses with colors unique enough or integrally associated with a brand may take the extra steps to secure a color trademark, as in the case of the The Coca-Cola Company's famous red.

Font

Whether you decide to go the path of a custom **font** or pay to use one already available, identifying how your brand's text will look is part of the branding process. Fonts, also known as typefaces, can convey emotions and style just as easily as other graphics. Does a serif font (fonts with extra embellishments on letter branches) or a sans serif (smooth fonts without embellishments) work best? Perhaps a cursive or highly stylized font? Choosing the right font, or fonts, can either enhance or distract from your branding efforts, and you should ultimately base your decision on your business's culture and targeted buyer.

While not necessary for every business, you may find your brand requires developing a custom typeface or font. Custom fonts are more commonly found in bigger brands that are after a unique look and brand consistency, particularly in the transition between print and digital marketing. Using a proprietary font design will further set your brand apart and ensure that no other business's communications will look like yours. Creating a custom font can be an expensive undertaking requiring a designer skilled enough to create a font that works across all marketing channels.

Your Color Choices Can Influence Buyer Brand Reactions

Shades of blue suggest: security, dependability, trustworthiness, and responsibility.

Black suggests: sophistication, prestige, timelessness, and value.

Shades of brown suggest: natural, earth-like, simple, and durable.

Shades of red suggest: power, excitement, vibrancy, energy, and youth.

Shades of yellow suggest: optimism, light, warmth, positivity, and motivation.

Shades of pink suggest: fun, girlish, childish or, depending on the shade's vibrancy, sexy.

Shades of purple suggest: sophistication, creativity, mystery, and nostalgia.

Shades of green suggest: wealth, prestige, serenity, growth, nature, and health.

Shades of orange suggest: friendliness, vitality, fun, and playfullness.

White suggests: purity, cleanliness, soft, and nobility.

Shades of grey suggest: peace and calm.

Voice & Message

One of your best brand culture reflectors is your business's **voice or message**, which quite literally sets the tone in all communications. Voice relies heavily on buyer profile research and incorporates marketplace and geographic cultural influencers. Your goal should be to develop a voice that not only reflects your culture, but is completely embraceable by your buyer. Adopting a formal tone may not be the best choice when trying to reach pre-teens, for example. Conversely, a relaxed, slacker style may not be best when trying to reach high-level professionals, such as lawyers.

Developing an effective voice may require integrating cultural trends, buzz words, jargon, or slang that present an impression of speaking your buyers' own language, or at least close to their language. Caution should be taken to keep your voice respectful and above the ridiculous; there's a fine line between speaking your buyers' language and sounding like a phony. Buyers are quick to spot businesses that try too hard!

Sound & Smell

Businesses that draw buyers into their own space can find an investment in the right background music or aromatics financially rewarding. While not as commonly found in the corporate world, **sound and smell** identities can be strong brand influencers in the retail and entertainment industries by approaching buyers on two additional sensory levels. The use of brand specific sounds and smell can contribute to a complete brand experience, allowing your brand to 'envelope' buyers. Have you ever passed a Cinnabon storefront and salivated while smelling its tasty treats? That's branding.

Sounds and smells can be highly memorable, drawing your brand to mind when buyers next encounter them. They offer an additional advantage of allowing your brand to catch passers-by who may visually miss signage or décor branding.

Jingles

Jingles expand upon your tagline's style and story, taking it a step further through the addition of (preferably unique) music. Originally a radio star, jingles have found modern success within the television and video worlds.

Successful jingles combine all of the same traits as successful taglines: they're easily understood and memorable. The best jingles permeate buyers' audio senses, acting as infectious reminders of the brand's services and products. If your buyers find themselves singing or whistling your jingle, it has achieved its purpose.

Packaging

An extended form of branding used in the product world, **packaging** can present in two forms, pre- and post-purchase. Most packaging is pre-purchase used primarily as a point-of-sale driven branding and buyer enticement tool. This form of packaging calls out to buyers from crowded store shelves, reeling in her attention until the purchase decision has been made. Post-purchase packaging presents itself in product delivery and shipping design and can be an excellent way to strengthen a buyer's experience and brand loyalty.

tolchicesiong / Shutterstock.com

The right packaging can have a tremendous impact on your business's sales. Otherwise great products can fail with the wrong packaging and find re-birth with the right one. Brands that previously faded into store shelves can become market leaders with packaging that stands out and attracts buyers. When competition is fierce, packaging makes a difference.

McDonalds uses packaging to enhance buyer experience while providing information on its food and beverages.

Packaging, as a marketing tool, can take many forms. It can refer to packages that contain and protect your product while clearly presenting your brand, or refer to an identification system such as a label. No matter what style is chosen, your packaging should catch your buyer's eyes and both persuade and educate those who know nothing or are on the fence about your product. The type of product dictates package design. Some package styles showcase products while others hide or protect, creating a sense of intrigue and mystery.

Packaging should also give information about your business, if only in the form of a name, web address, and contact information. Any inventory tools such as Universal Product Codes (UPC) or legal requirements such as nutritional details or warnings, must be incorporated into your packaging design. Packaging should always follow the brand guidelines set forth in your business's style guide (discussed later in this chapter). If your products are managed under their own business verticals, they will require their own style guides.

Décor brands your business's space in buyers' eyes. For example, there's no mistaking an Apple store with any other brand's retail space.

TonyV3112 / Shutterstock.com

Décor

Applicable more in the retail, entertainment, and destination industries, **décor** will theme your brand down to the tiniest detail. Using your buyer and marketplace profiles, research data, and with your business's personality as a driver, your brand's décor will come to life through the use of colors, materials, space layout, signage or art, decorations, and more.

The goal with décor is to create a complete brand experience through visual and tactile choices. Using a specified décor style ensures brand continuity in multiple locations, allowing buyers to instantly recognize a space as your own and have a strong inkling as to the type of experience your brand provides. The Walt Disney Company is a master at décor and theming throughout its many parks and stores.

Developing A Style Guide

No branding process would be complete without a guide for future usage. Known as a **style guide**, or branding guide, this document is the Bible when it comes to working with your business's brand. It clarifies what is acceptable brand usage and will help even the least informed employee use your brand properly. Having a style guide in place allows you to hold brand continuity across your projects, no matter the design source. Without it, confusion and personal taste by user can take over, thereby erasing the hard work that went into developing your brand in the first place.

Style guides typically include information such as color types (PMS codes, opacity screens), fonts and font sizes (broken out by headlines, sub-headlines, copy), logo placement, logo usage on backgrounds (i.e., reverse on dark background, color on white background), messaging, approved photos, and more. These brand tools are laid out within the style guide for ease of use and understanding.

A style guide will allow future designers and suppliers to know exactly what is and is not acceptable when working with your business's marketing

Consistently branded packaging allows products to stand out—or hide—on store shelves.

projects. Without it, you're giving them free rein to interpret your brand and how it should be presented to your buyers.

The implementation of a style guide is a good excuse to institute a business-wide purge of old branding components. Removing these components from daily access can alleviate off-brand usage in the future.

More Than One Guide. Style guides can be created to address brand architecture needs and individual product or service lines. Business verticals, product, or service lines may be addressed within a main style guide or broken out into their own. If broken out, it's helpful to keep a master guidebook at your business headquarters as a quick reference tool.

Brand Journey / Brand Experience Journey

Understanding how your brand impacts buyers and the path by which they discovered and bought into your brand is invaluable, especially for businesses that are established or have hit a growth plateau. The exercise that traces this impact is known a **brand journey.** Using a mix of graphics and text reviews, brand journeys snapshot your brand's evolution and buyer impressions.

360b / Shutterstock.com

A brand journey explores a brand's evolution as a whole, or by individual element, such as with the John Deere logos shown here.

Brand Journey

A **brand journey** reviews your brand over a set period of time, typically from founding day through present time. It's a timeline, showing an evolution of logos and taglines, changes in color schemes or packaging styles, and business achievements or pivotal events. More involved brand journeys may show a morphing of products or services over time and identify variations in buyers and markets. Statistics can be included.

Brand journeys can be useful tools, especially if you're evaluating your business's performance over time (environmental factors should be factored in with this exercise). Much like a marketing cheat sheet, a brand journey's snapshot allows you to review your brand's past image and activities and compare them against your future plans. It's a quick look at what worked and what didn't.

Brand Experience Journey

A **brand experience journey**, on the other hand, evaluates your buyers' introduction, reaction, and relationship with your brand. Using market research, it shows individual buyer's emotional journeys prior to making a purchase or walking away. It's marketing's "if / then" review and allows your business to address future buyers' barriers to purchase before they have a chance to walk away. Brand experience journeys can be created for a brand overall or individual products or services.

Questions asked in a brand journey focus on how and why a buyer sought out a business (referral, search engine, marketing piece) and the emotional and practical questions she may ask prior to making a purchase. Example questions include:

- Is it the right product for me?

- Does it meet my needs?

- What are my shipping charges?

- Can I return it?

Your brand experience journey may evaluate the market as a whole, looking for purchasing trends (i.e., mobile vs. desktop, found it via social media, etc.) and any other noteworthy indicators that suggest your brand may need tweaking. They can help you create a buyer behavior profile and allow you to hone in on what does and what doesn't work in your branding.

Brand journeys expose critical marketing information such as the paths by which a buyer sought out your brand. Was it from a blog recommendation? An advertisement? A loyal customer? These results can then factor into future marketing efforts and budget allocation.

Why Re-Brand?

Your business has undergone changes, some subtle, some grand, from the moment it moved past initial concept and became a fully formed legal entity through today. Sometimes it's necessary to refresh or completely re-brand a business to keep it current. Time may see a change in your business approach, structure, products or services, markets, or buyers, etc., perhaps resulting in a completely different business altogether. Outside changes in trends, buyer shopping styles, economic influencers, or perception may change your business for you. Or worse, incidents or negative press could have damaged your brand directly, resulting in business losses.

Re-Branding can breathe new life into an outdated or damaged brand. In a re-branding situation, your business has the opportunity to address a brand that no longer reflects its position, claim, or audience due to changes, good or bad, within the business, marketplace, or buyers. There are no shortcuts with re-branding; the steps for re-branding are the same as with initial brand development, and should include new market research and an updated marketing strategy.

Re-branding is expensive and disruptive, but it can save a failing business with an image issue (not an operations issue. Those won't go away with a re-brand). Re-branding can be a healthy exercise for a business that brings it up to modern times. It's also an excellent excuse to reach out to buyers and launch new campaigns and promotions!

Implementing Branding: A Unified Effort

Installing a new sign or ordering new business cards isn't branding's stopping point. For it to be effective, branding must be embraced by everyone in your business. After all, it's the public face of your business and the reflection of a business's personality. Branding happens regardless

Branding should be implemented throughout your business. Planet Hollywood's business exterior is as heavily branded as its interiors, making its building easily identifiable in buyers' eyes.

of what tools you put in place and negative branding is very real. It's a far smarter move to direct your brand activities than risk having buyers invent a potentially negative brand image on your behalf.

Branding exists in all business levels and buyer encounters. If an employee or department decides to use a different logo in a proposal, for example, or a sales attendant has a sour face while wearing a company shirt, the brand will be negatively affected in buyers' eyes. Some businesses will undertake a re-brand, but leave old pieces in place to "run through stock," confusing buyers. Buyers are less inclined to make a purchase when confused, resulting in lost business. The rule with branding is that everyone in your business is in it together, and for a brand to be successful, it must be integrated throughout.

Protect My Brand

Once you've taken the extraordinary steps to create your brand, you'll want to explore ways you can legally protect it. Much of this work may require the assistance of a lawyer who can walk you through your legal options. The following are a few of the ways you may be able to protect your brand:

Copyright. Any original work created by you, such as a design or article, should be copyrighted. This will prevent anyone else from copying or displaying your work without your prior permission. More information on copyrights can be found on the United States Copyright Office's website: www.copyright.gov.

Trademark. Although it can be a trickier process, trademarking your business name, tagline, or unique product or service names will prevent others from legally using them in business. More information on trademarks fan be found on the United States Patent and Trademark Office's website: www.uspto.gov

Domain Names. By purchasing your business, product, or service names in the form of a website domain (and all possible variations and extensions), you'll prevent anyone else from using your business name as a web address. Potential domain name availability is easily checked on any number of registration companies such as GoDaddy.com. I'll cover domain names in greater depth in Chapter 4.

Need To Know: Branding Opportunities In Your Business

Is your business doing everything to maintain consistency in your brand image? If branding is to work, it has to be an "all-in" effort that permeates an entire business. The following are branding opportunities you may find within your business:

Logo. Ensure that all logos used are current and follow your style guide. Make sure no one uses distorted graphics or off-brand fonts in business efforts.

Tagline. Do all of your marketing materials use the current tagline?

If your business uses different taglines, are they used appropriately and matched with both buyers and marketplace?

Sound. Have you sent out approved soundtracks or brand-approved satellite radio stations to your business locations? Are they played at appropriate levels? If not owned by you, have you secured usage rights when specific sounds are used in marketing efforts?

Color Scheme. Are you using the same color scheme throughout your marketing efforts? Are the colors on brand and consistent with your PMS color guide?

Fonts. Are all of your outward-facing messages written in the same font? This applies to more than marketing, and should include letters, invoices, etc. whenever possible. The exception must be made for government-mandated styles, as is the case with Requests for Proposals (RFP) or Requests for Information (RFI) bid packages.

Imagery. Have you identified approved imagery and photos that best represent your brand? If purchased, have you secured the correct license? Are you screening for unapproved images to ensure brand continuity?

Content. Does your marketing use the same voice and communications style throughout all marketing efforts from websites to business cards?

Interior Design. Does your brand carry through to your lobby, meeting space, and other publicly accessible office spaces? Is your logo / company name visible? Are walls painted in theme (or in a complementary shade)? Are your spaces decorated to match your guide?

An important note on interior branding. Special care should be given to your furniture, décor, and visible office space. Dated, banged up, or mismatched furniture do little to present a professional, thriving image in a buyer's mind. Dirty windows, chipped paint, cluttered desks or reception areas visible to buyers should be cleaned up. Bathrooms should be clean and inviting, not scary. Old magazines, faded pictures, or dusty awards suggest a business that can't be bothered with its image, which leads to the question, how could it care about its buyers' needs? Too many businesses try to conduct deals in stark, dated board rooms that double as a broken furniture repository. Will that setting inspire a sale?

Exterior Design. Does your exterior sign reflect the current brand? Is it in great, not just good, shape, with sharp paint and, if lighted, all bulbs in working order? Is your building's exterior clean, easily seen, and inviting? How about the grounds? Is the landscaping well kept and the parking lot accessible and in good repair?

Uniforms. If you have business shirts or uniforms, are they clean and fit your employees properly? Are they vivid or faded? Do they have the correct logo and colors? In professional settings, are shirts tucked in?

Truck / Car Wraps. If your business has delivery cars or trucks, are they fully branded? If not, this is a missed opportunity as these vehicles are, quite literally, mobile billboards. Any wraps, signs, or painted designs should be on brand and mindful of the old adage, "less is more." Your business's name, tagline, website address, and phone number are the minimum pieces of information. You may also consider locations and a few key graphics. Don't clutter up the wrap so much that your message is lost or hard to read!

Phone Messages. Have you created an on-brand script? Both receptionist messages and after hours recordings are excellent opportunities to reinforce your brand with buyers. The messages shouldn't be long or cumbersome, rather, a punchy nod to your brand will suffice.

Invoices and Forms. Are your business correspondences branded? It's far easier to convert a current buyer to a new service or product than to start from scratch with a fresh buyer. Therefore, branding routine correspondences such as invoices and forms is an easy opportunity to grow a current relationship.

4. I Think I Need A Marketing Mix

The best plans, brand, and budget in the world won't help you reach your growth goals if your buyers never hear about your business! This is why choosing the right mix of marketing tools is the next step in your marketing program's development. Reaching out and staying in front of one's buyers is imperative if your business is to thrive. Enter **marketing communications**.

Developing Your Marketing Mix

In decades past, determining the right **marketing mix**, particularly for smaller businesses, was more easily achieved. Ads in local print directories and the newspaper, a nice billboard sign, postcards in the mail, radio spots and maybe a quick TV mention, were standard and effective fare. Oh how times have changed!

Today's marketing world includes a wealth of digital and traditional vehicles. Our old standbys haven't disappeared, but some have been overshadowed by flashier opportunities that can address buyers quickly and directly. Interestingly, businesses have embraced new opportunities so wholly that many of the old standbys seem fresh and new in comparison.

The key to successfully selecting your mix is in matching your targeted buyer audience with engagement opportunities and resources. Not every opportunity is as it seems upon first glance. For example, a small, discounted space in the wasteland of an advertisement-heavy publication with few readers but heavy distribution (more on that later) is hardly a bargain.

As with any marketing activity, remaining on brand and consistent in message is critical. To be successful, your marketing mix must combine individual marketing opportunities that compliment each other in style and voice.

Need To Know: Minimal Marketing

While marketing is a custom activity, there are basic tools each modern business needs. This list doesn't include an outward communication vehicle, meaning that a minimal marketing program will rely heavily on networking and word of mouth.

Marketing Strategy. How can any business grow without a plan and a brand?

Name, Logo, And Tagline. Brand basics.

Handout. More than a business card. This could be a brochure or a simple handout card.

Website. Clear, easy to use, ideally professionally created using modern technology.

Multi-Channel Marketing

Multi-channel marketing involves spreading a message via more than one marketing opportunity. This could include sending a campaign through direct mail, digital advertising, signage, or just about any mix possible. Multi-channel marketing efforts can be scheduled for release at the same time to announce a special event (such as in a movie's premier) or spread out and staged over time as part of an ongoing marketing message.

The advantage with multi-channel marketing is two-fold: more buyers will see your message, and those same buyers will see your message more frequently, further cementing it in their minds. For this reason, multi-channel marketing should be every marketing campaign's starting goal.

Content

Buyers are drawn into and remember stories. They remember businesses that gave them information, helping them solve a problem or meet a need. In marketing, brand storytelling and the dispersal of free knowledge is collectively known as content, which is found in everything from blogs to videos. **Content** knows how to draw in buyers, speaking to them in your brand's voice while finding ways to relate your brand to their pain points. It's skillfully written, eager to help, subtly manipulative, and shares your brand's message in such a way that buyers won't soon forget.

Content isn't new, but its allure to buyers has made it one of the most talked about marketing tools today. Why? Because content gives message bombarded buyers something in exchange for their attention. More specifically, content directly addresses buyer needs.

In the landmark April 2011 study, "The Zero Moment of Truth Macro Study," by Google and Shopper Sciences, it was found that buyers are increasingly using research to guide their decisions well ahead of making an actual purchase. This holds true in both online and in-store purchases. The study's results are staggering: 88% of buyers consult an average of 10.4 sources before making a purchase!

Findings like these put added pressure on marketing, which has responded with an increase in content's quality, availability, and breadth. The driving force behind content creation is to earn buyers trust by giving them valuable information so that they return time and again—and bring their friends. Content's power lies in buyers seeking it out, then appreciating your brand's helping hand. Have you ever researched a problem online and found yourself watching a video or reading an article that solved your need? That's content at work.

Articles, helpful videos, informative social media posts, blogs, news alerts, infographics, seminars, webinars, podcasts, and so on are all considered content. Content can also be found in marketing materials such as a well written brochure that's more about giving buyer aid than bragging about your business.

Need To Know: Creative Terminology

Before breaking out the many marketing options available, I first want to share the creative terminology you're most likely to encounter while developing your mix. This will help you make sense of the many creative components that go into marketing projects. For instance, not all creative files are interchangeable, and understanding when each is appropriate will save you frustration and challenges down the road. Typical creative terms you'll find in marketing include:

Graphics

Resolution. The quality and cleanliness of a graphic's visual edges. Often expressed in dpi, or dots per inch. The more concentrated the dots, the higher the dpi number, the higher the resolution number.

Graphics are categorized as either vector or raster.

Vector Graphics

Vector graphics are completely scalable graphics that never lose image quality. Shrink a vector graphic down or blow it up, the quality will remain the same. This is due to their construction, which is a series of interlocking paths with defined start and end points and additional points at every shift in direction. These points can be moved and resized yet remain unchanged. Curves, straight lines, and shapes are all constructed of paths in vectors, which is what makes this an infinitely elastic graphic type. Also described as resolution independent. Photographs are not vector graphics.

Graphics that should be created in vector format include logos, fonts, and brand graphics. Vector file types include:

- **.EPS.** Encapsulated Post Script. A flexible file format that's the most commonly used vector format. It can gather information from both vector and raster graphics, therefore it's not a guarantee that a .EPS file is 100% vector.

- **.AI.** Adobe Illustrator. Software used in drawing vector graphics. Can be used to create almost any graphic project.

- **.SVG.** Scalable Vector Graphics. .SVGs are .XML (web) based vector graphics. Useful in web and animation.

- **.PS.** PostScript. A vector-generating programming language.

- **.PDF.** Adobe Portable Document Format. Highly versatile, can contain almost any type of data and can be created to work with printing presses and digital readers alike. Useful with larger documents.

Raster Graphics

Raster graphics. Much like a Georges-Pierre Seurat painting, raster images are constructed from a series of dots, or pixels, that are easy to see close-up, but create an image when viewed from afar. Set in a grid, these individual pixels seem to blend together when an image is small, then slowly spread apart as the image is enlarged. This gaping is known as pixelation or a loss of resolution, and once achieved, is there forever. Raster graphics are not scalable. They are some of the most commonly encountered images and are often used in digital work.

Graphics often in raster format include web, photo, and presentation graphics. Raster file types include:

- **.JPG.** Joint Photographers' Expert Group. Will always show a full rectangular background, usually white, whether your graphic has one or not.

- **.BMP.** BitMaP. Named so because it's a collection of image bits used to form an image. Digital cameras and scanners may produce .BMP images. These are large files that are often converted to another file type for use in marketing efforts.

- **.PNG.** Portable Network Graphics. Used in web and digital files because it maintains a clear background.

- **.GIF.** Graphics Interchange Format. A well supported bitmap graphic format used extensively on the web.

- **.TIFF.** Tagged Image File Format. Used for raw bitmap graphics. Scanned items are often presented in .TIFF format.

Other Graphic Terms You Should Know

- **.PSD.** Photoshop Document. A layered graphics file used by Adobe Photoshop software in everything from web graphics to print components.

- **PMS.** Pantone® Matching System Color showing pre-mixed print and digital colors by code number and color mix (RGB or CMYK)

Print vs. Digital Color Mixes

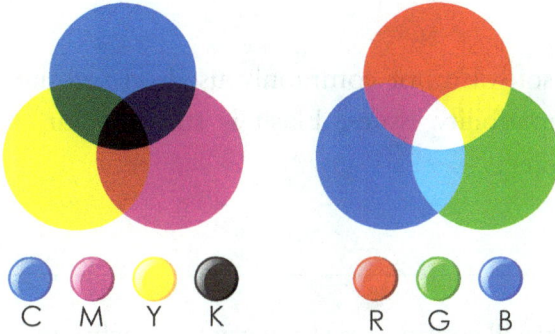

C M Y K   R G B

- **RGB.** Abbreviation for digital display color mix (web and presentations): red, green, and blue.

- **CMYK.** Abbreviation for the four process colors (print): cyan, magenta, yellow, and key (black)

- **Grayscale.** A graphic stripped of its color data that's shown only in shades of white and black.

- **Duotone.** A two-colored image rendered by layering one color over another.

Web Terms

Web development and design terminology will undoubtedly change in the future as new technology becomes available. There are many programming and coding terms used in the industry; however, these are the ones you're most likely to encounter in today's marketing.

- **.JQRY.** JQuery. A form of JavaScript that simplifies and eases client-side tasks on the web, such as animation and manipulating HTML, speeding up a site, and helping it work across multiple web browsers and devices, including mobile.

- **HTML5.** HyperText Markup Language 5. The fifth version of HTML released in 2011, HTML5 is the industry's standard markup language used to construct and present web content.

- **CSS.** Cascading Style Sheets. Language used to describe the look and format of a website.

- **.XML.** EXtensible Markup Language. A rule-based data carrying language. Used to carry rules for online construction and content information.

- **Adobe Flash.** An older software not commonly used on websites today due to mobile compatibility issues, Flash is still popular in graphics and animation projects.

Video Terms

As with web, video terminology will continue to change as new technology is introduced. The following are the file extensions you'll most commonly encounter in marketing today.

- **.MP4.** Moving Picture Experts Group 4. A digital multimedia format useful for video and audio files. Its high quality combined with compressed file size makes it good for streaming over the web.

- **MPEG4.** An MP4 file specifically encoded for video.

- **MOV.** Apple QuickTime Movie. Proprietary Apple video format that uses .MP4 within Apple's Quicktime program. Windows users must use QuickTime to watch .MOV files, making it less desirable for the web.

- **.WMV.** Windows Media Video. Proprietary Microsoft video compression format. Mac users must use an outside program to watch .WMV files, making it less desirable for the web.

- **.FLV.** Flash Video. Videos created for the web that must be played using Adobe Flash Player. Not as common as it once was as advances in technology have left Flash behind.

- **.AVI.** Audio Video Interleaved. Another Windows product, .AVI is designed to sync up video and audio data.

Graphic Files by Project Type

Logo: Keep original version in .EPS or .AI vector formats. Use .EPS in print or for promotional gimmes. In digital, use .PNG for a clear background or .JPG if a white background is okay.

Brochures, Postcards, and Handouts: Create in a professional layout program like Adobe InDesign. Can be sent to the printer as a press-ready .PDF or packaged file with all graphics and links. Single page files can be created in programs like Adobe Illustrator and should be sent with embedded graphics. Anything printed should be at least 300 dpi.

Advertisements (print): Print advertisements should be created in a layout or professional graphic program like Adobe InDesign, Illustrator, or PhotoShop. Send print advertisements as a press-ready .PDF or packaged press file. Printed advertisements should be at least 300 dpi.

Advertisements (digital): Static digital advertisements should be created in a program like Adobe PhotoShop. Send digital files as .JPG or .PNG files. Digital at 72 or 150 dpi. Animated advertisements may be animated GIFS or Flash files.

PowerPoint and Keynote: Use .PNG graphics for a clear background, .JPG for photos. Graphics should be 72 or 150 dpi.

Digital & Website Graphics: Use .PNG if you need a clear background, .JPG if the graphic will be applied to a white background. Digital should be 72 or 150 dpi.

Signs & Trade Show Graphics: Best created as a vector file using Adobe Illustrator to conserve file size. Some sign printers may request .EPS or even a full-size .JPG. Files should be at least 300 dpi.

Advertising

Long the backbone of marketing programs everywhere, **advertising** instantly conjures up images of swanky 1960s agencies putting creative spins on hand sketched campaigns. The advertising world is a little different today, but the constants of research, buyer profiling, demographic data, placement, and strong visuals coupled with equally strong copy haven't changed one bit.

Advertising's advantage is in potentially reaching a large number of buyers through a single effort. The downside is that, while it can yield tremendous results, advertising is one of the priciest marketing tools available, making it one of the quickest ways to blow a marketing budget. It's also an area where consistency is crucial as single ads, particularly smaller ads, seldom provide enough business to justify their costs. Success with advertising depends entirely on well designed, 'large enough to be noticed' advertisements consistently placed in researched and targeted outlets. Anything less is a waste of money.

Advertising can be extremely expensive, no matter the media outlet chosen. Generally speaking, price per placement directly aligns with the number of eyes or ears your advertisement will reach plus the quality of the buyers reached (targeted, not general). Television tops the list with multi-million dollar Super Bowl spots the crown jewel, but sticker shock can be found in all media by those not familiar with the advertising process.

No matter the media chosen, there are basic rules for purchasing ad space that apply whether you're after a business card sized print ad or are buying out a popular website. Always look at who and how many buyers the media outlet draws, then carefully, and realistically, calculate the percentage of buyers who could potentially see your advertisement. Keep in mind that size, timing, placement, and the media outlet itself will all factor into your advertisement's potential viewer number.

Types Of Advertising

Today's marketing mixes have a wealth of advertising opportunities available. Found in both traditional and digital media, advertising has the opportunity to reach large numbers of buyers in a short amount of time. Each form comes with its own layout and file requirements, production costs, and distribution options.

Print. Print media has been a go-to advertising resource for centuries, with newspapers and magazines leading the way. Newspapers offer high volume readership within a specified geographic region, (nationally, in the case of papers such as *USA Today* or the *Wall Street Journal*). Magazines target buyers with specialized interests and are generally distributed nationally and internationally. Print media spaces, known as display ads (as opposed to classified), are measured in column inches where the number of columns spanned equals the width and the inches equals the height. Special sections cost more and price is determined by size and placement.

Website. Online media outlets, blogs, websites, and e-commerce stores use advertising in a variety of ways, often bracketing their own content with advertisements. Web advertisements can be calculated by impressions (the number of times an advertisement will be visible on the site), by click-throughs that lead to another site (ideally, yours), by sales generated by the click through (affiliate sales), by placement and saturation within the site, or any combination of the above. Measured by pre-set space sizes with names like leaderboard, skyscraper, tile, pop-up, and background, website advertisements are always calculated in pixel width and height.

Pay Per Click. A form of online paid advertising often found on a search engine's results pages. Advertisements are auctioned off at a price paid per click and are tied to keyword search phrases. Different from online ads that are calculated in impressions, you'll only be charged for a pay per click advertisement when someone physically clicks on it.

Social Media. Popular social media outlets like Facebook and Twitter have been steadily decreasing their organic reach options in favor of sponsored ads and posts. As each social media outlet works toward a more lucrative structure, your business will have to allocate more and more budget just to reach your followers. Advertisements are offered by page and individual post promotions and calculated to reach a set

Choosing the right air times and channels will play a large part in your radio advertising's success.

number of buyers per campaign budget.

Radio. A throwback from advertising's earliest days, radio can still be a great way to reach buyers, especially during peak drive times. Advertising "spots" are calculated in duration and air-time, with :15, :30, and :60 second spots as the most commonly employed. Drive times and popular radio shows are typically the most expensive advertising periods. Satellite, web-based, and podcasts fall under this same general heading.

Television. The grand dame of advertising budgets, television spots command high price tags and heavy production costs. Like radio, television advertising "spots" are calculated in duration and air-time on a specific channel or station, with :15, :30, and :60 second spots as the most commonly employed. Highly rated shows (as by Nielsen's TV ratings) on popular channels are the most expensive option.

Billboard. One of the first forms of advertising, signs and, more specifically billboards, are found next to high population density and transportation routes all over the world. These types of advertisements do best in close geographic proximity to their touted business locations or sales outlets.

Directories. Once a business must, directories, particularly print directories, are phasing out of everyday life in lieu of the easily accessed online search engine. There are still important ones here and there, usually in conjunction with a specified group or traffic profile, including heavily trafficked online directories. Advertising opportunities are generally calculated by listing size and type.

Unusual. Advertising can also be found in unusual places such as stadium signs, popular email lists, bathroom stalls, restaurant menus, grocery store bags, event programs, and much, much more. It's important to evaluate each in terms of cost per eyeball or ear.

Rate Cards & Media Kits

The advertising process always begins with a rate card or media kit. These summaries of a particular media outlet's advertising program will give you the basic ad sizes and orientations available, costs per run involved, deadlines, file specifications, and placement options within the media, including special sections, ad formats accepted, and bundling options. Rate cards should also provide you with statistics on the media's distribution, reach, average shelf life (magazine vs. newspaper, for example), typical buyer, and any special publications / shows / opportunities throughout the year. With digital advertisements, you'll also see lines on costs per impression, (i.e. cost per set of eyeballs that may glance over your ad) and costs per click or click through rate (CTR).

Evaluate The Match

It's up to you to evaluate each advertising opportunity as a best match with your business. Be sure to read rate cards critically as they're designed to give you media-specific statistics while subtly influencing you to make the purchase. They are, after all, a form of marketing!

Carefully look beyond the fluff and evaluate if the media's readers and viewers fall within your buyer profile. Ask questions to get the information you need. Most media outlets will assign an account executive to handle

Need To Know: Advertising Layout Styles

Calculating Print Ad Sizes

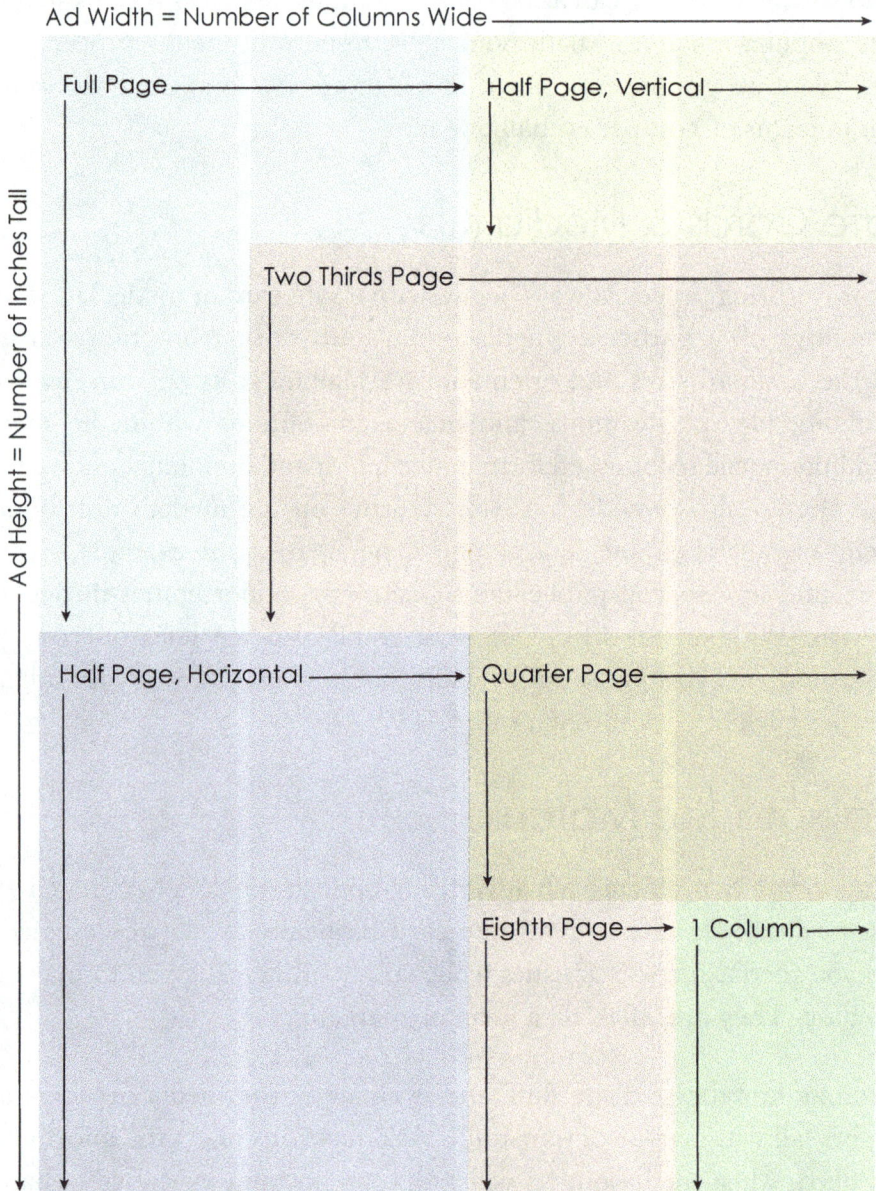

Ad Width = Number of Columns Wide ⟶

Ad Height = Number of Inches Tall

Full Page ⟶

Half Page, Vertical ⟶

Two Thirds Page ⟶

Half Page, Horizontal ⟶

Quarter Page ⟶

Eighth Page ⟶ 1 Column ⟶

Number of columns will vary with media outlet. Above is a 4 column publication.

Typical Digital Ad Sizes

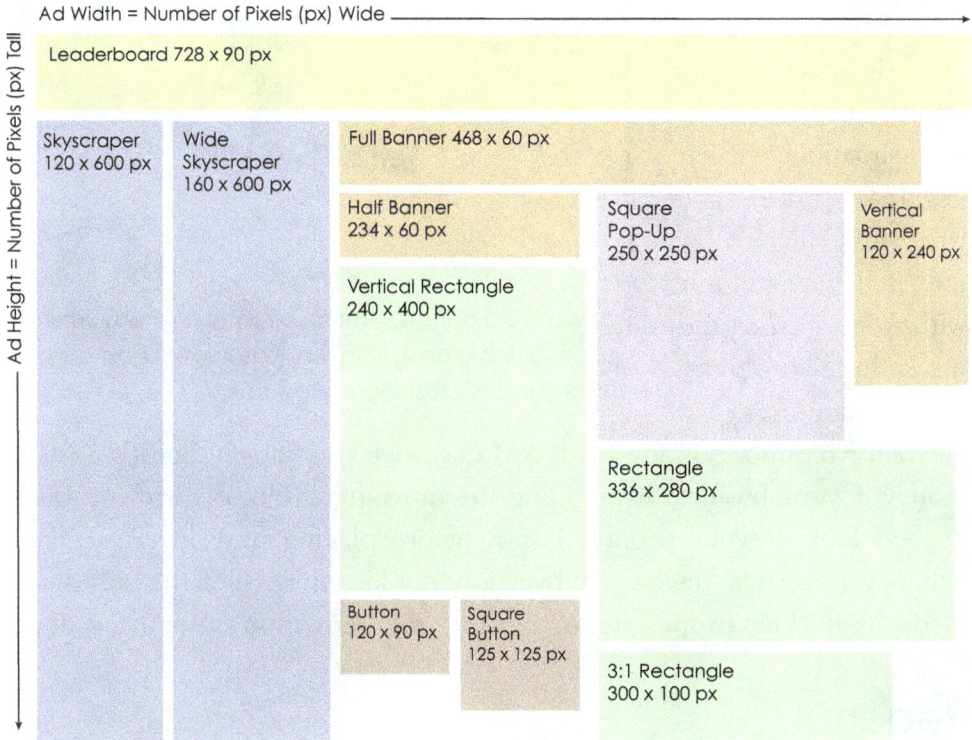

Ad Width = Number of Pixels (px) Wide ⟶

Ad Height = Number of Pixels (px) Tall

Leaderboard 728 x 90 px

Skyscraper 120 x 600 px

Wide Skyscraper 160 x 600 px

Full Banner 468 x 60 px

Half Banner 234 x 60 px

Vertical Rectangle 240 x 400 px

Square Pop-Up 250 x 250 px

Vertical Banner 120 x 240 px

Rectangle 336 x 280 px

Button 120 x 90 px

Square Button 125 x 125 px

3:1 Rectangle 300 x 100 px

your questions and advertising placements. Confirm that you're comfortable with the fit before placing any advertisement. Fit is extremely important — a magazine with three million women readers is virtually worthless as an advertising outlet if its average reader only earns $45,000 annually and your business is selling haute couture clothing.

Placement

As with real estate, advertising is all about location, location, location. This applies to both digital and print **placement**. Prime advertising spaces may cost more, but there's a reason and, in advertising, that always translates to potentially more eyeballs seeing or hearing your advertisement. There are situations where less than prime spots will work nicely, but only if they're still a fit with your brand and marketing program. For example, an

Some media outlets offer more than one advertising option, as is the case with the *Washington Post* and its online version, WashingtonPost.com.

inexpensive radio spot aired at 2 AM may save you budget, but it's wasted money if your business is targeting the morning commuter crowd. Take a good look at your proposed spot before placing any advertisement. Whenever possible, review a full version (not kit snippets) of the published media itself. That proposed spot may look different upon closer inspection.

Reach

Reach refers to a media outlet's distribution and market penetration. It can be calculated by evaluating a media outlet's geographic distribution or in the number of people who read, view, or listen to it, on average or in a set period. Reach often changes by days of the week, times of year, or hours in the day, and can be influenced by distribution channels. Examples of changes in reach can include the difference between Monday and Sunday newspaper readership, a new market signing (or dropping) a television channel, or the winter holiday issue of a home decorating magazine compared with its summer issue. Be sure to check a media outlet's reach on the days and times you wish to run your business's advertisement, or you may find a smaller audience on the receiving end.

Run

Run simply means the length of time your advertisement will spend with the media outlet. In print, this means the number of insertions or number of publication dates within which it will be placed. In digital, this means the number of impressions or the number of days visible, or both. Run is broken out by time periods (three ads in a month, 12,000 impressions within 24 hours), and will usually include a discount with increased frequency.

Advertising's effectiveness depends upon buyer retention, and few people notice and remember an ad from one viewing or listen. Even a poorly crafted ad can become memorable if run often enough (although its effectiveness may be questionable). In other words, your ad should likely run at least a few times if you wish to see a return on your investment.

Production Costs

It's worth noting that any advertising rate is only a portion of your business's advertising costs. Production costs, especially in television and radio, can be as much or many times more than the cost of the space itself! Media outlets have strict guidelines on what formats and file types they will accept, which many businesses find often requires outside supplier help. A full page advertisement for one publication, for example, may not be the same size and proportions in another, requiring additional work from your designers.

Production costs are part of what makes advertising such an expensive endeavor. It can be a effective way to reach large numbers of buyers, but many smaller businesses may find themselves locked into shorter runs or smaller spaces, purely due to budget limitations. Your production decisions shouldn't be made with an eye toward saving advertising budget. After all, the cost is the same to run a bad ad as a good one. You stand a better chance of seeing a return with a good one.

Media Buyers

With larger campaigns or cross-market campaigns, it may make sense to bring in a **media buyer** to help coordinate and secure the best advertising spot pricing. A good media buyer should have at least some personal contacts within major media outlets, allowing for quick pricing and schedule turnaround. It's this person's job to find the best possible advertising options within your targeted marketplace and suggest a schedule when your advertisements will have the best chance of reaching your buyers. If you're working with a marketing or advertising firm, it may have this person in-house. If not, this person should be considered an outside consultant with rates entered into your advertising budget.

Direct Mail

Direct mail has evolved dramatically over recent decades with the advent of email and a push for more environmentally friendly marketing efforts. The obvious advantage to direct mail is its direct access to a buyer's home or office, catching her via the mail or inbox. Too many businesses competing for the same buyers has led to overloaded inboxes and mail fatigue, which means that for a direct marketing piece to be effective, it has to be eye catching, clearly present a value, and look or feel different enough to snag more than a cursory look.

Past direct mail staples such as solicitation letters, postcards, brochures, gimme packages, newsletters, and flyer drops have had to share space with email blasts and e-newsletters. While these all qualify as forms of direct mail, they differ from each other in execution.

Print

Once the gold standard in direct mail, print has lost marketing favor to email in the last twenty years. The saying, "everything old is new again" applies to print direct mail pieces as fewer businesses employ this direct mail option. With less physical mail hitting mail boxes, your opportunity to

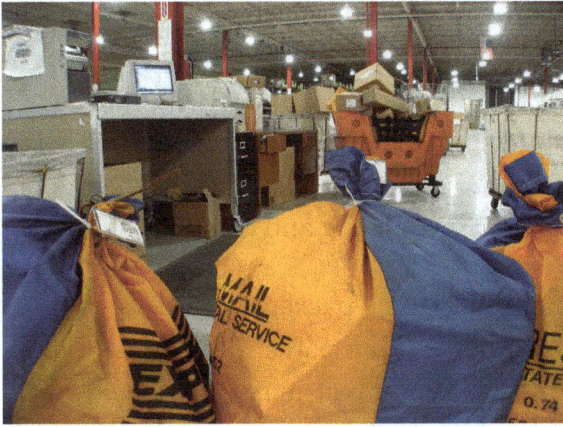

Print direct mail, especially bulk mail, must conform with the USPS's specifications.

stand out with print direct mail has never been better. Standing out is the key descriptor in direct mail. Your piece, and message, must be eye catching!

Print direct mail does have its own limitations and rules. More to the point, your post office's rules. Self-mailers such as postcards and newsletters must conform to the post office's size and layout specifications if you want to keep rates to a minimum. The United States Postal Service (USPS) houses a list of its mail requirements, rates, and templates on its website, www. USPS.gov.

Direct mail isn't limited to postcards and newsletters. Gifts, product kits, mailed promotional items, surveys, etc. all fall under direct mail. Postcards are typically the least expensive option. Personalization can be achieved through variable printing methods, making it easier to speak directly with your buyer, even customizing content and calling her by name. Standard direct mail classifications, include:

Postcards. Postcards are rectangular, single pieces of paper, usually of a heavier card stock, printed on both sides, and sent without an envelope. Your design must comply with the USPS's layout requirements that include designated blank areas for delivery use. USPS postage is calculated by size height, length, and thickness, with a minimum of 3.5 inches high by 5 inches long and a maximum of 6.125 inches high by 11.5 inches long and .25 inches thick.

Letters. Letter campaigns may be sent in single or multiple sheet formats, shipped within an envelope or folded and secured with an approved tab.

Letter-sized direct mail is useful for more than actual letters. You'll find flyers, surveys, invitations, tickets, announcements, and more can be sent this way, as long as your pieces fit within standard USPS letter guidelines of a minimum of 3.5 inches high by 5 inches long and a maximum of 6.125 inches high by 11.5 inches long and .25 inches thick. Larger, flat envelopes must not exceed 12 inches high by 15 inches long and .75 inches thick.

Parcels. Product, press kits, and promotional packages can be sent under the parcel classification. Ideally, you'll send out parcels to a smaller, more targeted mailing list because this form of direct mail can be expensive. Minimum parcel sizes are 3 inches high by 6 inches long and .25 inches thick. Maximum is calculated by overall size at no more than 108 inches in height and length, combined. The maximum parcel weight is seventy pounds.

The marketing downside to print direct mail is that it can be difficult to track results. This is why every piece you send out should include some trackable call to action such as a special offer code, unique web link, or mailable response card (with pre-paid postage). Otherwise you may find it tough to determine your print direct mail campaign ROI.

Bulk Mail

If your plan is to send a campaign to a large mailing list, you'll want to explore **bulk mail** shipping rates. Less expensive than first class, bulk mail is ideal for uniformly sized and structured campaigns such as postcards, letters, or newsletters.

New users may find bulk mail's restrictions tough to follow, but these rules, layout, and sorting limitations are what keep this shipping option more affordable than first class.

Bulk mail postage is tracked through a printed indicia (shipping mark) rather than a stamp or meter-run postage. It's possible for businesses to purchase their own indicia; however, unless you're planning to routinely send large runs of bulk mail, you may want to avoid the extra headache and use your printer's.

It's tempting to use bulk mail as a way to reach buyers frequently. Too frequently, in fact. Anyone who has received candidate postcards during political election seasons knows that there can be too much mail from the same source.

Email

Considered a more affordable form of direct mail, **email** has become the dominant direct mail format in modern day marketing. This is largely due to its lower delivery costs, speed of delivery, connection with your business online, and tracking options, making it the easier choice for quick and direct communications. Postcards can become e-blasts, and newsletters digitized and sent as e-newsletters. The challenge with email is in breaking through inbox clutter and technology safeguards.

Cost is email's most attractive quality. While production and design costs still exist, shipping prices can be significantly less than print mail, with each email costing as little as $.01 per delivery. Depending on your chosen delivery service, your emails can be tracked real-time, allowing you to see how many recipients have opened and clicked through to linked sections of your website or a landing page. Recipients who have unsubscribed should be visible, allowing you to better evaluate your list, message, or delivery frequency.

As with print direct mail, successful email campaigns rely on quality execution, buyer value, and engagement. This is not only a sound marketing practice, but also an investment in remaining compliant with the CAN-SPAM Act discussed later in this chapter. Email is broken down into two categories:

E-Blast. Typically a single message email that can be an announcement, invitation, introduction, or information request such as a link to an online survey. E-blasts can be structured as simply as a mass letter requesting a meeting or as complex as a full graphic sale announcement. E-blasts are always sent to groups in a mass mailing.

E-Newsletter. Similar to more traditional newsletters in their mix of stories and business news, e-newsletters generally offer multiple information bits linked to longer stories on a business website. This form of email is content-driven, usually offering recipients knowledge in exchange for their time.

Delivery Methods

Email can be sent in text format, graphic format, or a mix of the two. While plain text emails have an easier time navigating spam and security filters, they can lack the pizzazz of a graphics-based email. On the flip side, emails heavily laden with graphics can be too busy for your buyer's attention and have a higher risk of never making it to her inbox at all. Regardless of the type you've chosen, you'll want to test your email on as many different systems as possible before sending, and structure it to be no more than 600-800 pixels wide and a minimal amount of scroll length.

Determining the type of email you're sending out will also guide the design process. Generally speaking, your graphic emails should follow a 1:3 ration, with up to 25% of the email as graphics and the remaining 75% for text and blank space. HTML graphics tend to fare better than embedded or attached graphics as email services are wary of potential viruses and label these emails as spam. With HTML emails, you must house the graphics online somewhere, either on your own business website or through an email service. The image is really sent as a link, greatly reducing the size of the email and likelihood that a filter will catch it. Recipients will need to enable "view HTML" settings on their email systems.

Once you have your design in mind, you'll want to select your delivery vehicle. Your in-house email system is usually a poor choice as most standard systems aren't designed to send emails in blocks greater than fifty without triggering a negative flag on the recipient's email system. You could go through the extra time and expense of setting up and managing your own email platform or purchasing email software, but in many cases this isn't necessary.

There are many excellent online email services such as MailChimp®, Vertical Response, and Campaign Monitor that will help prepare and test your email before you send it out. These services typically offer tracking data, allowing you to see how many people have opened, clicked on, and unsubscribed. With these services you can use a pre-set template or upload your own fully branded email and email list. Your mailing list will need to be uploaded as either comma separated values (.csv) or tab delimited values files.

If you decide to send out a smaller e-blast through your personal email account, remember to add recipients names in the 'BCC' field, not the 'TO.' Sending out a mass email with all recipients' addresses visible is a fast way to tick people off.

CAN-SPAM Act

In 2003, the United States enacted a law affecting all electronic mail communications. Named the CAN-SPAM Act, the law is enforced by the Federal Trade Commission and "sets the rules for commercial email, establishes requirements for commercial messages, gives recipients the right to have you stop emailing them, and spells out tough penalties for violations." Details of the law and its applicability to business can be found on the FTC's website, www.ftc.gov, but the gist is that all advertising or promotional email must be clearly and obviously messaged, with no bait and switch subject lines or headers, and offer recipients an easy opt-out (unsubscribe) option that's absolutely honored by the sending business.

Frequency

Using direct mail can feel like walking a tightrope strung between buyer awareness and buyer tune-out. Send out too few mailings and your message may be lost or forgotten. Too many and you run the risk of annoying buyers and having them tune-out your brand. The best path is to start somewhere in the middle and allow recipients to determine how often when they sign up. Whatever you decide, consistency is key.

It may be tempting to send out massive amounts of direct mail to your buyers, but restraint is key, particularly with email. Unless buyers have signed up for frequent communications such as daily or weekly news updates, two to three print mailings and one to three emails spaced adequately per month is a more than ample number for most businesses. Send any more than that and you'll see your "unsubscribe" numbers climb rapidly.

Developing A Mailing List

Your mailing list should be thought of as a living document that will increase over time. You may add to your list one person at a time or purchase names from an organization or mailing list service. The strongest lists are developed using "opt-in" techniques where buyers subscribe to your mailing list. Opt-in points can be housed on your website, purpose-built landing pages, social media, or through in-person meetings. It's tempting to request copious amounts of information in your opt-in forms, but you'll have a greater likelihood of signing up a recipient with only an email address field.

There are times when a purchased mailing list makes sense. If you're trying to reach a targeted membership, draw attendees to your exhibit at a trade show, or are breaking into a completely fresh market, a purchased list can offer your business a leg-up. More often than not, you'll only have the option to use the list on a rented basis, and may have to send your direct mail through the service that gathered the recipients through its own opt-in format. In purchased list situations, part of your direct mail's message should include a "subscribe now" call to action.

Collateral

A catch-all term for business informational handouts, collateral includes brochures, rack cards, pamphlets, tri-folds, sales slicks, folders, etc. Like many other print projects, collateral's role has changed in the last twenty years, and today it's hard to imagine a time when businesses printed massive, ten to twenty page collateral pieces, with detailed pages on services and products. Websites have done away with much of this need, allowing for quick updates and easy access; however, most business owners find that there's still a need for a professional handout piece. Handouts are an opportunity to put a piece of your business's brand directly into a buyer's hands. The sizes may have changed, but the role has not.

Why is collateral still a business mainstay? There are two primary reasons:

1. Having an extra memory point after a conversation or event encounter helps to further cement your brand in a buyer's mind, easing follow-up.

2. Handouts can promote your business without your presence. They can be left on counters or racks, placed in hotel rooms or swag bags at events, or distributed by buyers and strategic partners.

Some buyers like having a product or service list as a reference for later use and will often spring from a handout to a website as the next step in pre-purchase research. Even better, they'll take your handout and share it with other potential buyers. Wouldn't you prefer that your own content sell your business in that situation?

Collateral Types

Brochure is the catch-all term for a multi-panel document that showcases your business, a product or service line, or both. Long considered a marketing mainstay, brochures today tend to be smaller, more focused, and dependent upon buyer friendly content. They're less of a business showcase and more of an opportunity to resolve your buyers' needs. Brochures can take many forms, all using variations on a folded page. Your business use will dictate your brochure's style and size.

Page or panel counts are always calculated in even numbers due to folding and stitching requirements and are limited in overall size by the size of your printer's press. In other words, if you'd like to add a page or panel to an existing brochure type, you'll actually have to increase the overall brochure by two (in panels) or four (in extra pages). Not all presses can handle larger sheets of paper, meaning that one of your brochure's measurements (usually height) is limited to that maximum paper size.

No matter what brochure style you land upon, you'll want to opt into the nicest, heaviest **paper stock** you can afford. Buyers associate the quality of your brochure's paper with the quality of your business. It's perfectly possible to maintain an environmentally friendly image with today's recycled and sustainably sourced paper stocks, discussed in greater depth in Chapter 6.

Brochure Formats

Bi-Fold. Bi-folds can be a single sheet folded in half, resulting in a 4-panel brochure, or a single sheet with additional pages stitched (usually saddle-stitched, or stapled along the edge)

Tri-Fold. A single sheet folded into three panels, resulting in a 6-panel brochure.

Gate Fold. A form of tri-fold, where both outside panels fold inward and meet halfway across the middle panel, resulting in a 6-panel brochure. These can be dramatic and work well with invitations or destination businesses.

Multi-panel. A single sheet folded into a set number of panels. These can have additional pages stitched inside. Options are almost endless, but you'll always end up with an even number of pages and panels.

Handout Formats

Single sheet handout cards are an inexpensive way to provide business information. These typically have information on both sides and are printed on heavier stock. These cards can be printed vertically (portrait) or horizontally (landscape) in orientation, depending on your need.

Rack Card. A narrow card designed to fit into rack displays. Standard rack card sizes are 3.5 inches by 8.5 inches and 4 inches by 9 inches.

Handout Card. Printed on heavier, thicker stock and usually smaller than an 8.5 inches by 11 inches sheet of paper.

Sales Slick. Typically used in folders and sales packets, sales slicks are printed on lighter stock, often a 8.5 inches by 11 inches sheet of paper.

Flyer. A single sheet handout or advertisement. Often a 8.5 inches by 11 inches sheet of paper.

Common Brochure Layout Styles

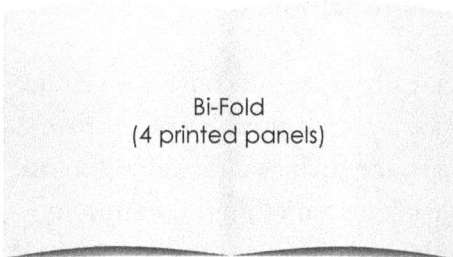

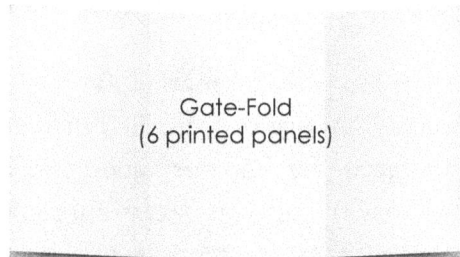

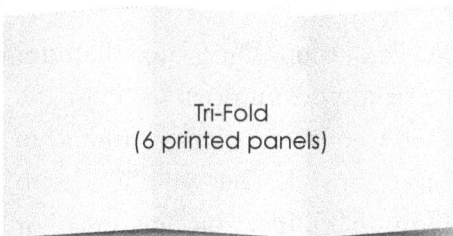

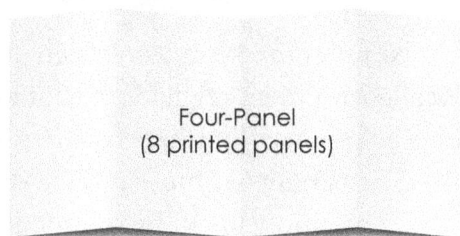

Bi-Fold
(4 printed panels)

Gate-Fold
(6 printed panels)

Tri-Fold
(6 printed panels)

Four-Panel
(8 printed panels)

Door Hanger. A handout card designed with an opening cut out of the top, large enough to slide over a door handle.

Signage

Signage is the most basic of all marketing tools. Signage can say, "my business is right here. Right here, turn now." It can tower above busy streets, causing passers-by to look up at your brand or stay close as they sit, waiting for a train. Signage, or signs as they're commonly known,

Busier locations, like Times Square, are perfect sign and billboard marketing opportunities.

Stuart Monk / Shutterstock.com

can lead buyers to your business in a series of small bites or scream that your business is having a sale right from your front window.

Signs are physical marketing tools strategically placed in buyers' eyelines, usually on heavily trafficked or densely populated routes. You may own a sign, as in one on your building, or rent a space such as a digital billboard. No matter the type, successful signs always have one thing in common— impact. The message is always clean, simple, and obvious. They're designed to catch attention very quickly.

Unlike other marketing tools, signs, specifically outdoor signs, can fall under local government regulation, either on the size, type, number, or all of the above. You may find your business restricted to only one sign or limited to fixed signs only (vs. more mobile directional signs). It's best to check with your local government before spending too much budget on new signs, or

Point of sale signs draw attention directly to their products.

you may find yourself with a pile of useless marketing dreams.

The types of signs generally encountered in marketing include:

Storefront. Used exclusively on the outside of your business, storefront signs let buyers know that the location is yours. Storefront signs come in all shapes and sizes, using a wide variety of materials that range from back-lit acrylic to hand-lettered images on glass. Usually these types of signs are limited to your logo and tagline.

Advertising. Found throughout the world, advertising signs are a part of every urban landscape. The most commonly thought of sign is a billboard, which can range from simple painted wood and canvas to a more sophisticated digital screen. Dramatic, backlit advertising signs may show full color, graphic, or photograph-focused messages and are commonly found at transportation points like airports and entertainment centers like stadiums and shopping malls. Mobile signs are almost always on the move and are found on transportation vehicles like buses, trains, or on wrapped cars and trucks. Advertising signs fall under many of the same advertising rules discussed earlier in this chapter.

Point of Sale. Used exclusively in situations where a buyer can make an immediate purchase of the touted product or service. Point of sale signs are used to grab a buyer's attention and entice her into an impulse or add-on purchase. These types of signs can be large and bold, commanding retail square footage, seemingly casually placed on a table-top or counter, or small and affixed directly to a product's shelf.

Event. Designed to further enhance an event experience by promoting features, special events or add-ons, or helping guide attendees and guests through the event itself.

Directional. Locally focused, these signs are used to lead buyers to a specific destination. They can be found as a series of small bandit signs on the side of a road, spun by an active guy at a busy street corner, or held in place by temporary stake posts. These signs are extremely useful for special events and sales or if your business is difficult to find.

Digital Media

While the basic approach driving digital marketing mirrors traditional, this ever-evolving, technology-based world has its own set of rules and terminology. **Digital media** is grouped into three different media types: paid, earned, and owned, and most successful marketing departments employ a combination of all three. While this book won't delve into the daily management of this ever-evolving world, I do want to give a high-level overview of these three media types. Keep in mind that each will require continual investment and daily management.

Paid Media

Exactly as named, **paid media** is, fundamentally, a form of advertising situated alongside unpaid information. Paid media allows businesses to promote themselves through placement in areas buyers may feel are informative and organic. Paid media can be fast and highly effective and, in some forms, both expensive and labor intensive. Similar to traditional forms of advertising, if conducted improperly, paid media can also be an area where money spent doesn't necessarily result in a high return.

Grouped into this category are search engine placement purchases such as Google AdWords, search engine optimization (SEO), online directories, social media ads, and pay per click campaigns (PPC).

If you wish to tackle paid media in-house, you may find yourself facing a steep and frequently shifting learning curve as algorithm changes or new players throw off your results. You may decide to outsource this work, in which case your consultants should be carefully screened as this area is rife with claims that can differ wildly from results.

Pay Per Click

Also known as cost per click (CPC), **pay per click** (PPC) media links your online advertisement to your website or landing page, leading to a direct connection between your buyers and business. It's as simple as the title suggests; you'll pay the media or search engine each time your ad is clicked by a web user.

Depending on the PPC source, you may have to bid on the amount you're willing to pay per click. Based on this, it might seem that a larger budget will win the day with PPC, and larger budgets can lead to results seen almost immediately; however, you'll need to keep close tabs on your results to prevent overspending. In fact, you may find that you're paying more to win PPC than you're receiving back in revenue. In all cases, results should be tracked by conversions and relevancy, otherwise PPC campaigns are an exercise in blindly spending money.

There is no guarantee with PPC that each click will be made by a potential buyer, which can result in a budget drained by worthless clicks. Moreover, unlike traditional advertising where run can help decrease cost over time, there are no frequency breaks in PPC. The price is the price, no matter how many times your advertisement is clicked.

Google AdWords

Google AdWords may be the best known form of PPC media. Google AdWords uses its own platform that capitalizes on its own search engine and selected keyword search phrases rather than a designed advertisement provided by your business. Other popular search engines like Bing and

Google AdWords

Google AdWords displays paid advertising listings across the top and right side of its search windows. Listings in the left-hand column are organic, or unpaid, results.

Yahoo have similar PPC programs. Advertisements are structured on four lines:

- the first a bold, 25 character headline

- followed by two, 35 character description lines,

- and the last, a 35 character display URL line.

Google AdWords advertisements are sold auction style via a maximum price paid per click, per keyword phrase. Advertisements are locked to a series of keyword phrases, grouped in a campaign. A **keyword phrase** in this case means the exact words you expect a potential buyer will type into Google that could lead her to your business. You may run multiple campaigns at once, each focused on your own products and services and using a unique set of keywords. If your business is in multiple locations, you may choose to run a series of local campaigns, or campaigns in other languages to match your national or international efforts.

Crafting your set of keywords requires research and careful evaluation of results over time. Google offers a free tool, its Keyword Planner, that will help you develop your keyword list, but you should also closely monitor your own results and determine what works best for your business. Long-tailed keywords phrases such as "beehive seller in Lexington Kentucky" may give you more precise results, but may also limit your options.

Because Google AdWords are auction-based, you'll find that more popular keyword phrases can command higher bid prices. Bid amounts can be increased as competitors clue into key phrases. Budgets per day will limit the number of times your advertisement is displayed, and your campaign will run until either your predetermined budget runs out or a set period of time ends.

Affiliate Programs

Another version of PPC is **affiliate marketing**. Affiliate marketing is a form of PPC, in that you'll pay another business a commission on sales made by clicking on your advertisement housed on that business's site. Designed to work with e-commerce sites, affiliate marketing can be rewarding to all parties involved, your business as the advertiser, the website that hosted your advertisement, known as the publisher, and the buyer herself. You received a sale, the publisher a commission, and the buyer found out about a product or service that satisfied a need. A win-win-win. . . Or is it?

Using web cookies that engage when a buyer clicks on your advertisement, affiliate publishers earn commissions as a percentage of buyer purchases. This sounds fantastic on the surface, but like other forms of PPC, affiliate marketing can become highly competitive. Competition drives commission percentages up, resulting in your business losing money. Unscrupulous practices by some have given affiliate marketing a bad reputation in the recent past, and care should be taken when considering a publisher or affiliate firm. Unfortunately, affiliate marketing's past advantages as an SEO link builder disappeared with a change in Google's algorithm, eliminating what marketers had viewed as a commission off-set.

In affiliate marketing's best cases, your advertisement will stand out, appear as an endorsed product or service, and deliver quality buyers. In the worst, it's simply another message cluttering a site for which you pay a high commission. If yours is an e-commerce site, affiliate marketing could be an amazing traffic driver, but with the understanding that the rules for vetting any advertising opportunity discussed earlier in this chapter should be applied before you sign an agreement.

Your business can participate in affiliate programs as an advertisement's host. By allowing affiliate advertisements on your site, you're able to take a cut of the affiliate pie without advertising your own products or services. Some popular blogs allow affiliate advertising as a replacement or addition to a traditional display advertising program. Google has its own version in Google AdSense, which displays Google selected advertisements on websites, mobile sites, video, and games. Before allowing advertisements on your own site, first ask if they'd enhance your brand in your buyers' eyes.

Setting A Budget

Common sense and a careful evaluation of your results should dictate your PPC budget. Each campaign must offer a ROI or there's little point in continuing the effort! Often the best course of action is to ease your way into PPC while constantly monitoring your campaigns, looking for areas of improvement. If you're spending more than bringing in, it's time to make adjustments or move onto another marketing tool.

Search Engine Optimization

One of the most frustrating and elusive forms of paid media is **Search Engine Optimization** (SEO), primarily because it's one of the most difficult to control and manage. At first glance, SEO may not seem like a form of paid media, as its goal is a higher ranking within organic, or unpaid, search results. The ultimate goal is to be the first listing on the first results page when your targeted buyer keys in a business-related search. It's achieving this unpaid ranking where you'll incur expense in time and budget. SEO may be segmented into overall and local search engine plans that work together.

The challenge with SEO and its sister activity, **Search Engine Management** (SEM), is that search engines such as Google, Bing, Yahoo, and Ask.com change their algorithms, or how they calculate rankings, regularly. This is both to prevent shady, 'blackhat' manipulations and to fine tune the search process. Rankings achieved by satisfying a previous algorithm's requirements could be shuffled down under a new calculation. Fortunately or unfortunately, depending on your point of view, there's no magical way to achieve high search engine rankings overnight, and attempts to game the system through antiquated practices such as link, meta tag, or keyword stuffing often backfire in today's rankings.

On the plus side, achieving higher rankings often involves good practice efforts your business should have in place anyway! Quality content, above-board linking practices, active social media accounts, newsworthy press releases, listings, reviews, and linked mentions on reputable sites all contribute to a better ranking. Search engines reward activities that appear to be of benefit to your buyers and that prove your website is a relevant (and legitimate) part of a specific business area.

Chasing search engine rankings can be taxing, in effort and financially. The decision to invest in an SEO consultant will depend largely on your budget, market size (SEO can be locally based), and business's dependence on search engine traffic. Be careful in your selection, as the wrong consultant could cost you a lot of money with poor to mediocre results. A best practice, particularly for smaller businesses, is to clean up your digital activity first and worry about search engine rankings second.

Social Media Advertising

The idea that social media is a free marketing tool is rubbish. True, it won't cost your business to set up a page within a social media channel, but simply setting up the account isn't enough to gather buyer likes, follows, and, most important, interaction! Gathering and engaging buyers through consistent content requires valuable time (something I'll spend a little more time on in the social media portion of this chapter), and, as more and more social media channels move to a paid for promotion model, budget.

Reaching your followers and drawing in new buyers organically is becoming more and more difficult as popular social media channels tweak their own algorithms to downplay promotional posts and encourage social interaction—and encourage paid advertisements. Any chance you have of reaching your followers' news feeds organically will largely depend on outstanding content and their own previous participation. Frustratingly, the percentage of organic reach is sadly quite low and continues to drop, particularly for business pages who want to push their products or services.

Consequently, social media paid promotions have gained popularity. Through paid promotions, you can push your page, a post or tweet, or even a trending campaign to your followers' feeds. Each platform offers slightly different rules surrounding their promotional models, but most base their campaigns on budget, duration, and your targeted set of viewers. Targeting an audience allows you to select demographic parameters like age, gender, and location, as well as special interests outlined by the user herself. There's usually a review period to ensure that your promotion meets that channel's requirements. Most frown on over the top promotions and may hold you to a less text more image graphic ratio.

Paid promotions have multiple benefits. Newly established pages can get a jump start on follower numbers by promoting their pages. Special events, new product or service announcements, sales, or news in general, can be promoted to a targeted audience. As with other advertising opportunities, you should base your activities on ROI. Monitor your campaigns. If you're spending a fortune yet only receiving a few quality followers, paid promotions aren't a best fit with your marketing program.

Owned Media

Owned media refers to anything created and controlled by your business. Original articles, videos, social media channels, in-house generated graphics, websites, blogs and similar are all considered owned media.

Websites

It's tough today to find a more important marketing vehicle than your website. Why? Because, barring a catastrophe, it's accessible 24 hours a day, seven days a week, from anywhere in the world, by anyone! It's the address listed on all your other marketing efforts and often buyers' starting point when researching your business. All online activities should connect back to your website. If professionally developed, your website should become your perfect marketing tool. Certainly it's tough to have a successful marketing program today without one!

Your website is an opportunity to immerse buyers in your brand, within a setting you 100% control. Your story, colors, and culture are all available at the click of a mouse. After your marketing strategy and branding program, your website will be your biggest marketing investment in terms of effort and money. Remember, your goal is to not only increase the number of buyers who visit your site, but also the amount of time they spend on your site interacting with your brand. Known as bounce rate, single page visits are evidence of a site that isn't engaging buyers.

As tempting as they might seem, beware the free or cheap website! As with discounted logos, you may find your site looks like many others and is built upon a dated platform. Buyers are quick to spot an unprofessionally designed or templated site. Both can project the image of a small, more 'mom and pop' business. This is not the image you want your buyers to have when interacting with your business and brand.

Behind The Scenes

Deciding what should be included on a website can be a lesson in economics. As a general rule, the more features on the site, the more expensive the project. A simple corporate site is considerably less expensive than an e-commerce site with a fully functional store front. Whittling down a list from the wants to the needs is the first step; however, the resulting site must always include the following key features for it to have any sort of impact:

Address. Securing an easily grasped and memorable web address is, quite literally, your website's starting point. Known as a **domain name** or **uniform resource identifier** (URL), this string of words is your website's Internet address, or how people will find your site. Your business should own its domain name. This address is a part of your brand and you should never let another business such as a web design firm hold your domain on your behalf!

Your domain name purchase is an annual expense separate from your hosting service. A change in file extension equals a different website address, such as is the case with website.com, website.info, website.biz, etc. Whenever possible, start with your business name and the .com extension and purchase as many variations as you can comfortably budget.

Hosting. A separate budget item from your domain name, hosting refers to the physical location where your website is housed on the web. Hosting options abound, and you may choose anywhere from an economic shared server through a dedicated server with a **Secure Sockets Layer** (ssl). Your anticipated usage and traffic will dictate what type of service you choose. A larger e-commerce site accepting credit card payments will need an ssl, whereas a small, local businesses could get away with a shared server. It's often a better decision to choose one of the larger hosting providers who have teams of people managing their systems rather than a discount provider that's less stable and accessible, should you need help. Your choice in hosting service can have a direct impact on your website's speed (and buyer reaction) and whether it stays up and running at all times.

Once you've chosen your hosting service, you'll need to have your domain name directed to it. If you purchased hosting from a different service from your domain name, the redirect process can take 24-48 hours as the entire Internet must be notified of the change. This external timeline applies no matter what service provider you choose.

If you pay a web design firm to host your site for you, it may actually be hosting it through a third party provider at a fraction of the cost. I advise businesses to seek out their own hosting with a larger hosting service as it could end up less expensive, technical service is probably free, and your site won't be held hostage should your designer relationship sour.

Platform. One of your earliest website decisions will surround your website's structure, both behind the scenes and public facing. Every website is constructed out of a series of code that dictates component actions, style, and placement within the site itself. This code could be written in a variety of programming languages you'll probably never need to know, such as PHP, JavaScript, Python, to name a few, and your choice of platform will largely dictate how your site will be constructed.

Businesses wishing to make edits and updates to their own sites will want a form of **Content Management System** (CMS). CMSs are a What You See Is What You Get (WYSIWYG) programming platform that allow you to add, modify, delete, and publish portions of your own site without knowing how to code. One of the most popular CMSs available is WordPress, but there are others like Drupal and Joomla, or you can choose a proprietary CMSs created by a web development firm. The advantage to using one of the more popular platforms is that they typically are lower in cost and have a vast number of available add-ons consistently hitting the market.

Format. Are you looking for a more traditional, multi-page site or would you prefer a single, scrolling page with menu anchor points? There are advantages to each, and your decision will boil down to personal preference and business type. One page sites can offer ease of use on tablets and mobile phones; however, today's responsive programming allows multi-page sites to have a similar scrolling structure. Multi-page sites allow for menu sub-pages, easing navigational woes on larger sites. Take a look at how much information you need to put on your site and determine which version will work best with your business.

Responsive vs. Mobile

Mobile devices and the number of buyers using them as web browsers has made web design with these devices in mind a marketing priority. The need is so great that businesses lacking a mobile presence may find themselves losing business. Buyers frequently skip or jump from sites not optimized for their devices.

There are three ways your business can handle its mobile website need. The first is to create and maintain a separate mobile site designed entirely around mobile devices. The second is to use responsive technology in your website design. The third is to use adaptive design. Your budget and access to a dedicated web team will dictate which option you choose. Most smaller businesses find responsive web design fulfills their needs nicely.

Mobile Website. Mobile design is just that, web design crafted entirely for mobile device browsers. A stand alone mobile site is structured using mobile-friendly programming and screen specifications, resulting in a mobile-optimized site. The disadvantages to this structure include the cost of creating and maintaining an entirely separate site on top of your main site and in meeting the demands of the growing tablet market, which are devices not served by mobile or traditional sites. This option requires a separate mobile URL in addition to the one used by your main site.

Responsive Web Design. Responsive websites are constructed using programming that automatically adjusts the site's layout to fit various screen sizes. In other words, the site will automatically and seamlessly expand and contract to look its best on mobile phones, tablets, desktop computers, or laptops, without the visitor having to click or adjust anything. This is a crucial technological advance as more and more web shoppers use mobile

Responsively designed websites automatically adjust to fit various devices and screen sizes.

and tablet devices. The disadvantage is that some responsive programming can load a little more slowly as the entire site must be downloaded first, then re-sized according to the device used. Responsive websites use the same URL throughout.

Adaptive Web Design, on the other hand, is built upon a series of pre-set layouts that are set for different screen sizes. The advantage to adaptive web design is that your site is optimized for its predetermined size and will load more quickly than responsive design. This happens when your web server determines what type of device has made the request, then loads the appropriate layout. The disadvantages are in the cost of creating so many layouts and in maintaining the technology when new screen sizes enter the market. Adaptive web design uses the same URL throughout.

Website Components

While developing your website, it's important to make sure key components are included and, if applicable, easily found by your buyers:

On Brand. There's little point in going through a full branding process if your most visible marketing tool isn't on brand. Using your style guide as a reference, your website should showcase your brand's color scheme, fonts, approved graphics, style, and tagline in a clean, approachable manner.

Navigation. Visiting a website with buried information and poor navigation is a frustrating experience that buyers tend to avoid. Why risk a buyer leaving your site quickly because the information she needs is hard to reach? Easy, straight-forward, accessible navigation will go a long way to helping buyers engage with your site.

Content. Content in terms of your website refers to the text that collectively tells your business story plus any photos, white papers, videos, blog posts, or other informative pieces buyers can access. Your content should be written in your brand's voice, keeping in mind that you're trying to satisfy a buyer need while enticing them to make a purchase. Your content should keep SEO best practices in mind, namely, using a clear keyword identifier, focusing on a specific topic (per your keyword), and including more than a sentence's worth of information on each page.

Call To Action. Your site should always include a call to action that provides buyers with an easy next step activity and path by which they can reach you. Your type of business will influence what type of call to action you use, but many sites use some form of a "contact," "more information," or "purchase now button." Requesting that visitors subscribe to your email list is another form of call, as are sign up forms for upcoming events or webinars. Having an enticing call to action will not only engage buyers, but also provide tracking information on your website's performance.

Social Media Links. Any social media links actively maintained by your business should be connected to your website via an icon or channel feed (or both). Buyers should have the option to share content, especially blog posts and articles, via on-page social media share buttons.

Tracking. How will you know when, how, by whom, and from where your site is visited without adding a tracking component? Through collected data on your site, you can track your site's performance over time, allowing you to make educated improvements and build visitor profiles. There are many tracking options available, ranging from free through expensive subscription services, each offering a different tracking approach and resulting data. I'll cover tracking again in Chapters 7 and 8.

Content

Your website will be an empty space without content! This collective terms refers to all copy, articles, videos, etc. that help tell your business's story while engaging buyers and helping solve their needs. Good content is developed with buyer needs in mind, using your brand's style and voice as its guide. I don't mean that you shouldn't have business information and details on your site; rather, it's the approach and presentation of these details that's important.

Buyers are less likely to read page after page of business-based information unless it uses a "what's in it for me" style. By taking a buyer-focused approach, you'll improve your chances of creating a bond between your business and buyers—and winning over skeptics. It's important to remember that, as with branding activities, content isn't limited to that which has been well-researched and professionally created. Anything you create and post online is considered content. The question is whether or not it's good and effective content.

Therefore, it's important to look at each web element in terms of content. It's helpful to ask yourself if what you want to upload is educational, thought-provoking, of quality, timely, helpful, on-target, relevant, trustworthy, or inspirational? Is it on brand and in keeping with your buyer and market profiles? Does it paint your business in a positive light? More specifically, does your content:

Solve A Need? The best web content solves buyer needs through direct information, blog posts, video tutorials, infographics, downloads, question and answer lists, etc. Determining what needs should be addressed goes back to your marketing research and strategy, but can also be based on questions asked by buyers in social media, top search engine phrases, through forms on your site, in surveys, or just about anywhere that the question can be recorded and pulled by you or your team. If you pay attention, your buyers will tell you how you can help, and you can use this insight to flesh out and build your website.

Engage Buyers? Long data lists can be informative, but the likelihood that a buyer will spend much time reading them is pretty low. In other words, for your content to be effective, it also needs to be engaging and tell a story. Engaging doesn't mean novel-length or blockbuster film quality; it simply means that it can hold a buyer's attention and answer her need in a reasonable amount of time. Sometimes the most engaging content is quite short and answers only one question. The key to engaging buyers is not in the length, but in your ability to tell a story in an emotion-evoking, and memorable, manner.

Establish Expertise? Ultimately all content should support the idea that your business is an expert in your field. If not, what's the point of spending money on it? Your choice of content topics and the manner within which you present the information will tie back to your business's products and services. For example, if your business is selling video equipment, it makes sense that your content will be video-driven. If you're in a food-based business, some of your content might take the form of recipes.

User Experience

It's no secret that buyers tend to spend more time and effort on sites that are easy to use, informative, and clean in message. Enter user experience design. **User experience**, or UX, is the process of designing a website (or app) entirely by how it will be interpreted and used by visitors. At its best, it's a deeply involved, scientific process that leaves no stone unturned when evaluating the look and feel of a site. UX goes beyond simple design and content and delves into the details of experience, such as accentuating the ergonomics of a site to meet Americans with Disabilities Act (ADA) requirements. UX exists to better create an enjoyable, informative web experience.

UX can be a complicated field and is made all the more complicated to the average person by its many varied titles and methodologies. What most people need to know is that UX will pull a site apart by its components, then test, test, and test them to make sure everything flows in a user-friendly and optimized fashion. Using a process known as **iterative design**, UX follows a methodology of prototyping a site's design, testing its components and flow, analyzing any results, then making refinement changes based on

Simple E-Commerce Wireframe

NO.	ELEMENT	TYPE	DESCRIPTION
1	Login	Portal	Login & acct details
2	Search	Text Entry	site search
3	Logo	Area	Logo graphic
4	Shopping	Link	Link and amt
5	Shipping	Text	Shopping offer
6	Navigation	Main Nav	Drop down
7	Navigation	Links	Direct links
8	Content	Area Slider	Sales / product announcements
9	Social	Links	Direct links
10	Sign Up	Text Entry	Email sign up
11	Content	Area Slider	Weekly special Ad Slider
12	Content	Video	Product video
13	Content	Area Slider	New products Carousel
14	Content	Area Links	Inbound links
15	Navigation	Links	Footer links

Wireframes are one tool employed by UX professionals. These basic illustrations are used early in the process to lay out a website's elements and structure.

those results. Because it's a never-ending process, UX will always strive to move your site to its best possible version, incorporating technology, trends, or buyer changes over time.

While a true UX review by a senior professional can be very costly and involved, the business application of an enjoyable, informative site can pay for itself time and again. These professionals will break down your needs and develop a layout and structure that incorporates buyer behaviors and improves overall website experiences. UX activities are broken out by individual components that range from the psychology of design through page schematics to end-user behavior. If you have the time and budget, UX can help you create a better website experience.

Landing Pages

If increasing leads and conversion rates is important to you and your business, you'll want to incorporate landing pages into your website program. These pages are destination pages created to focus traffic on a single topic, event, or activity, thereby increasing interest and, ultimately, leads. They can be stand-alone or attached within your main site, and should draw buyer traffic on their own. Landing pages should be simple and singular in message, on brand with your business, and include a strong call to action, such as a sign-up or contact form.

The appeal of a landing page to your marketing program is in its simplicity. This is a controlled environment where your business can focus buyer attention on a single topic, using your content and call to action. Because landing pages focus on a single topic, they can be an asset to your SEO rankings, especially if the focus is based on your identified key word phrases. You may take the extra step and purchase a separate URL for the page or house it as a page within your own site. Including a visitor tracking method will help you determine ROI.

When are landing pages most effective?

Advertisement Destinations. Landing pages are of particular use with advertising campaigns, including PPC campaigns such as Google AdWords, because they have expanded information and details not available in the advertised offer.

Launches or Releases. Landing pages are perfect for upcoming events or exciting new product or service launches and releases. Countdown clocks, teaser videos, chapter downloads, buyer comments, and more all play into building excitement on landing pages.

Special Offers. Discounts, special promotions, giveaways, contests, and downloads are all ideal reasons to create landing pages. You can have multiple landing pages in place for the same offer, but promoted to a different audience. This will allow you to attribute response rates to different sources or use different pages to promote different offers.

Differentiating Buyers. Similar in motive to special offers, using landing pages to differentiate or segment buyers can help you hone your message to a buyer type's taste, then track response rates and returning buyer profiles. This is a useful approach when you're targeting different buyers with the same product or service. For example, if you're selling something like IT service packages, you could then target your message for a particular buyer type, such as office managers, IT professionals, and homeowners, through a series of landing pages.

Social Media

Social media is everywhere these days, with individuals and businesses alike promoting their handles and encouraging buyers to "follow," "like," or "pin" them. Social media immediately offers a direct connection between a business and buyers, available from anywhere in the world, 24/7. There are few other ways for buyers to reach your business CEO, the media, or investors in relation to a brand as quickly and easily than through social media channels! Despite this, social media can fail to produce actionable business results due to a lack of understanding, poor approach, or infrequent communications.

The reason businesses struggle with social media often boils down to a simple misunderstanding. Rather than embrace the *social* component of this marketing opportunity, too many businesses view social media as a soapbox from which they can push their own information and news. Business information is

Facebook is the biggest and most popular social media channel worldwide.

important, but it can't be the only content used! In fact, social media should follow content rules and answer the same questions regarding education, interest, relevancy, and timeliness. It should solve a need, engage buyers, and establish your business as an expert.

More than anything else, however, approach your social media posts with an understanding that whatever you're about to upload needs to interest your followers. If your business routinely engages in activities about which buyers clamor for information, by all means keep them informed through your posts! Even those types of businesses need to break up the monotony with industry information, news stories, videos, or behind the scenes photos. Few businesses can find success in social media by only talking about themselves.

As with any other marketing activity, keeping followers interested means staying visible. If your schedule only allows infrequent posts with large time gaps in between, social media is probably not worth your effort. Unfortunately, many businesses set up a social media profile only to let it sit and die by inactivity. Why would anyone want to follow a business that doesn't have enough interest in its own social channels?

While each channel has its own set of best practices, there are a few global rules that can be applied to all of your social media efforts:

Be Social. Social media depends upon open communication and the sharing of stories and ideas. It's an opportunity for you to speak and interact with your buyers and maintain a pulse on their questions and needs. Comments or questions need a quick response in a positive, professional manner. Pay attention to your buyers' concerns, and let them know someone is listening and values their opinions. Avoid arguing or fighting with people in social media!

Share The Love. It's irksome to come across businesses who like gathering followers, but who never (or rarely) follow-back or share others' information. Social media isn't "all about me" media. Follow-back, like, retweet, and share with buyers and other businesses. It only makes your business look better! If, for example, your Twitter feed shows nothing but your original Tweets, your approach is way off the mark.

Stay On Topic. While it may seem like your followers enjoy an endless stream of inspirational quotes or cat videos pulled from other websites, the reality is that your chances of gathering new business from these posts is extremely low. That is, unless you pepper them within a mix of relevant and informative posts. The content rules apply—keep your topics close to your own business's products and services and with your buyers' needs in mind. Setting up an editorial calendar will help you keep your social topics on track.

Each Channel Is Unique. Overlaps can and should happen on occasion, especially when you're running a campaign, but if your standard social media approach is to post one item and auto-push it to every channel, you're missing the point of a targeted audience. Each social media channel has its own unique style and audience, requiring slightly different messaging and post types.

Find Your Own Mix. Social media channel mixes are not universally applicable. In other words, what works well for one business may be a miserable failure for another. Find the channel mix that works for your business, not someone else's.

Allocating Resources

As I mentioned earlier in this chapter, social media is not a free marketing tool. It will cost your business in terms of time and design resources to properly set up and maintain it over time. While it may be tempting to have an intern or junior staff member register your business on every available channel, then post random items over a short period, this approach will do little to gain new business.

For your business to find success in social media, it will need to invest (by either hiring or re-allocating in-house time) in a responsible channel manager(s) who can post on-brand topics your buyers will appreciate; she should be experienced enough to answer any questions or comments in a mature and professional manner. This person will act as the voice for your business and needs to be up to the task. Too many businesses have found themselves digging out of a public relations hole created by a business spokesperson who inappropriately shared, reacted to, or commented on, social media posts.

In addition to securing a social media professional, you'll need design help to customize the look and feel of your social media channels. Each channel has its own specifications on logos, banners, and post graphics, and it's impossible to use the same graphic universally without re-sizing it first. The look and feel of your social media pages needs to reflect your brand, and if you don't have someone in-house who can create this work, you'll need to enlist a graphic designer's help.

Each social media channel will require basic information about your business in the formation of your channel page:

Category. One of the first tasks you'll have to address is selecting a business category. These are often broken out by industry then sub-category.

Logo. Your channel logo will become your business's icon attached to your posts and uploads.

Profile. Depending on the channel, you may write a few words or paragraphs on your business. Some channels, like Facebook, have room for both a short and long description.

Branding. Almost every channel will allow some degree of branding, be it as a wallpaper background, banner across the top of the page, or color scheme. Use your style guide to develop your social channel branding.

Website Link. Most channels will link back to your website. Some, such as Pinterest, will also verify the site and mark your channel as "verified."

Social Media Links. Some channels allow other social media links, either as direct access on your business profile page or through the use of social apps.

Products Or Services. Some channels, such as LinkedIn, will allow an additional product or service list that can be used as both a quick reference and in-channel search tool.

Choosing Your Channels

Choosing social media channels is no different from any other marketing project, follow your buyers and compare the investment with your potential ROI. With new social media opportunities springing up each and every day, the decision to create a new channel is one that should involve effort prior to securing a presence. It helps to view social media as you would an advertising opportunity that first requires research, evaluation, and matching up an audience with your buyer profile before spending money. A little time up front will save you wasted time and investment down the road.

The good news is that there's a right channel for every business and brand style. Questions you should ask yourself when choosing a channel:

- Are the channel's user profiles broken out by demographics? A channel skewed to a business crowd won't work if you're targeting teenagers.

- How will you communicate with buyers? What is the social structure? This varies widely from channel to channel, as can be shown by the difference between Twitter's 140 character tweets and Instagram's photo based posts. Is this communication method a fit with your business?

- How easily can you maintain this channel? Can you provide fresh, quality content on a consistent basis?

- How do followers see posts? If a social channel has revamped its structure to reflect a more paid, less organic news feed, as in Facebook's case, can your business afford it?

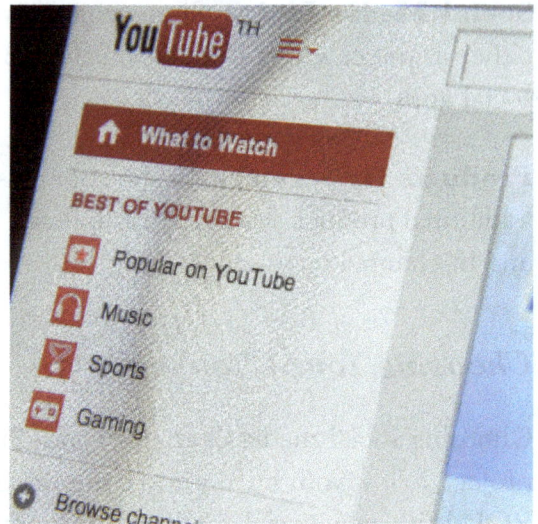

2nix Studio / Shutterstock.com

YouTube's dominance over video sharing makes it an attractive social media choice.

Today's most popular social media channels include:

Facebook. Currently the biggest social media channel; however, rumors abound about its decline as a business tool. It allows for full page branding, a wide assortment of posts from straight text through video, direct follower comments, rankings, apps, and offers group and chat capabilities. It has powerful targeting and reporting tools. Changes within Facebook's structure have hit organic marketing hard. Today's Facebook channel demands an advertising and page / post boosting budget lest your posts go unseen by the majority of your followers. It has a reputation of a more "friends and family" channel than news and business.

Twitter. Breaking news and communicating directly with your intended audience are the hallmarks of Twitter, making it an ideal content sharing channel. Despite its limitation to 140 character posts, known as **tweets**, Twitter users manage to say quite a bit and spread information quickly. Businesses use it to reinforce credibility and area expertise, as well as a fantastic customer service and announcement tool. The use of hashtags (#) allow for easy searches on specific phrases, and businesses have learned to draw in buyers with key #phrases. The downside is that tweets have a short shelf life and may be missed by followers. Twitter offers an advertising and reporting component that pushes tweets out to targeted users.

LinkedIn. The most business-focused of all the channels, LinkedIn is perfect for connecting with potential B2B buyers and future employees. Similar in posting structure to Facebook, it's best used for articles, business news, announcements, and opportunities. Sales teams rely heavily on LinkedIn for its relationship building and prospecting advantages. It's also a great way to push content out to a business-minded audience. LinkedIn offers targeted social group building tools that allow for collaboration, sharing, and recruiting as well as a blog posting service named Pulse.

Pinterest. A photo and video based social channel used overwhelmingly by women, Pinterest has found a home with businesses who can supply it with gorgeous product photos, how-to videos, infographics, and well-illustrated articles. Users can create themed boards which are then populated with image-based posts. Pinterest-wide searches can be conducted on key words. If your business can pull together beautiful photos attached to informative content, you'll love Pinterest.

YouTube. Videos, videos, and more videos are found on YouTube. This social channel is 100% dedicated to video sharing, and is a tremendous way to disperse how-to and business video content. Owned by Google, it easily connects with search results. It's not uncommon to have YouTube videos show up at the top of Google search results, making quality video an enticing marketing tool. Bear in mind that quality video is important to achieving success on YouTube, and that continuously feeding this channel can be an expensive undertaking in time, preparation, and filming costs.

Tumblr. Owned by Yahoo, Tumblr is a microblogging social channel that will allow you to post an assortment of content. This content is then consolidated into a short, easy to peruse, blog-like dashboard. Users can explore and follow others' blogs, and share just about anything web-compatible. Businesses with active blogs and heavy content-generation programs find Tumblr a strong social channel.

Instagram. A smart phone-managed social channel that's photo and video based, Instagram is best suited to businesses with fun photos and a youthful target audience. Because all photos must be uploaded via a smart phone or tablet app, Instagram is ideal for behind the scenes, 'capture a moment' content rather than pure business activities. It can be powerful as long as the photos uploaded to your business channel are in keeping with Instagram's fun-loving, youthful audience.

Worth Noting, Google+. Originally conceived as a Facebook competitor, Google+ enticed marketers worldwide with its search engine connections and social circle structure. 2015 saw major changes after Google dissolved its original social structure, eliminating the channel's mandatory connection with YouTube and a Google account and spun off some of its key features into what it calls Streams and Photos. The channel then launched its Google+ Collections, aimed at taking on Pinterest. It's relevancy as a social channel remains unknown as of this writing.

Posting Frequency

Setting up your social media channels is only the first step in the process. The next step is what I call "feeding the beast," otherwise known as setting up and managing your posting frequency. The volume and frequency of your posts will largely depend on your channel choices and targeted buyer, but it's fair to say that you should think in terms of a daily, if not multiple times per day, posting schedule.

This doesn't mean posting simply to post! Quality and relevancy should be the driving force each time. It's not hard to find examples of people who have high post but low follower numbers, which is a clear sign that there's little interest, or perceived value, in what that person is posting. If you can't consistently post quality content, it's time to re-evaluate the number of channels you're managing and whether social media is a right fit given your current resources. What does a quality posting mix look like? It's heavily skewed toward educational or entertaining posts (60-70%), with a smaller infusion of light business news (15-20%) and business promotions (15-20%). Sharing, liking, and re-tweeting from other sources can fall into the educational or entertaining category and should be an ongoing effort.

Once you have the resources at hand and are ready to get started, it's time to create a frequency schedule. Best posting schedules will vary from channel to channel, and what 'best' means often sparks debate among social media professionals. Since not every business can manage heavy posting requirements, I suggest a "just enough to stay relevant without annoying followers" approach. The following are suggested schedules for growing the most popular channels:

- **Facebook:** One to two times per day, mid-morning and early evening.

- **Twitter:** Three to five times per day, spaced out in your buyer window (see below).

- **LinkedIn:** One time per weekday, first thing in the morning.

- **Pinterest:** One to five times per day,

- **YouTube:** One time per week.

- **Tumblr:** One to two times per day, mid-day.

- **Instagram:** One to two times per day, morning and evening.

Your post schedule also depends heavily on your buying audience. For example, if yours is a local business looking to pull from your local market (and time zone), your **buyer window** is much shorter than, say, a business trying to reach buyers across the country or around the world. Those businesses will need to develop a much larger posting window that may include scheduling some posts in the wee hours of the morning. Furthermore, if your buyers are generally inaccessible or rarely on social media during certain time periods, you won't want to schedule posts during those times.

There are numerous tools that will help you develop your own posting frequency plan. Many social media channels have tracking tools in place that will let you see when your posts have the most success, and you should evaluate your results over time. These tools should help you determine what types of posts resonate best and encourage discussion with your followers.

Posting tools will help you schedule your social media activities in advance, which is a tremendous help during busy seasons and over weekends. Tools such as HootSuite and TweetDeck allow you to create multiple posts and schedule over days, weeks, or months. Some help manage postings across multiple channels and accounts.

Organic vs. Paid Reach

In an ideal world, all social media reach would be gained organically. **Organic reach** simply means that your followers, comments, likes, pins, etc. were earned rather than purchased on the social media channel. It suggests that followers discovered you through their own searches or found you through others's likes, comments, or follows. It's the best case outcome for any social media activity and what every strategy strives toward. Because it's earned, organic reach is a very powerful marketing tool and should be your goal with all social media posts.

Quality content and in-channel activity help boost organic reach and buyer interaction. The more on-target you are with your posts, the more receptive and engaged your buyers will be, and the more effective your social media efforts will be to your marketing program.

Unfortunately, pure organic reach isn't always possible. Changes within some social media channel structures has led to a more financial rather than altruistic model, resulting in decreased organic delivery. These channels have greatly reduced the percentage and types of followers who will see your posts organically to increase their own advertising revenue. Facebook has experienced the most dramatic shift over the years, and today it's difficult to build a new page within the channel without applying a boosting budget. In this situation, reach may be limited to those who have recently interacted with your page, leaving the rest of your followers with ample time to forget your brand.

Paid reach is exactly what it sounds like; likes or followers you've gained after boosting a post or your page. Paid reach offers targeted posting. Using the channel's boosting tools, you can craft a buyer profile through demographic and post habit data and reach a fresh and new audience. Paid reach is useful when establishing a new page, promoting an event or news item, or perking up interest heading into peak sales seasons.

Used in conjunction with an organic reach program, paid can be a beneficial marketing tool and should be viewed as a form of advertising. As with any advertising, care must be taken to ensure business value through tracking and ROI reporting. If you're paying to reach people who aren't your buyers, it's just another form of wasted budget.

Paid reach is different from buying followers from a fly by night, '1,000 followers for $5' outfit. Purchase those at your own peril as most social media channels frown on the practice and periodically clean up and remove fake followers. Not only is it a complete waste of effort to post quality content to fake followers, but it could be embarrassing for your business to have 10,000 followers one day, then 200 the next after a channel purging.

Blogs

Housed online and often incorporated within websites, **blogs** are powerful content generators geared toward drawing in buyers. Consisting of a series of posts that are published online, blog content can take form in a written article, video, infographic, or just about any informative and web-friendly and easily read data collection. Due to their informative and business-related topics, blog posts can be influential content contributors to the rest of your marketing program.

Do you really need a blog? Maybe. There's no doubt that a well-written, informative, and frequently updated blog can be a boon to your marketing program and qualifies as valuable content from both a buyer and search engine's perspective. A blog offers your business an opportunity to address buyer questions and needs directly, through carefully crafted content. For this reason, blogs can boost brand engagement and your business's image as an expert. As long as it's maintained! It's not uncommon for businesses to start a blog, only to let months, sometimes years lapse between postings. In this situation, having a blog is a negative to your marketing program as it will age your website, not enhance it.

Once you decide to tackle blogging, you'll want to develop a blogging plan that maps out what topics you'll cover and when. The best plan is to set up a blogging schedule (daily, weekly, bi-monthly, monthly) and stick with it. Whether or not your blog is a successful marketing tool will be based on how you apply the following:

- **Value.** Your blog needs to provide value to your buyers. This can take the form of news items, how-to and explanations, education, or entertainment. You shouldn't use your blog as a catch-all for quick business updates. That type of information is best saved for social media. Instead, approach blogging as a way to provide solutions to your buyers' needs, known or unknown, that they, in turn, will value.

- **Relate To Your Business.** While your blog should speak to your buyers, it also needs to tie back to your products or services because, again, what's the point of spending marketing budget if it won't bring in revenue? This doesn't mean creating sales pitches or product pages within your blog! Instead, choose topics that your products or services can solve. For example, if your buyers want to know about environmentally friendly practices in the home and you sell green cleaning products, you'll probably want to include at least a few blog posts related to green cleaning.

- **Timely.** No one wants to spend time reading outdated or commonly known information, so why would you waste time blogging about it? Pick topics that are timely and on (or should be on) your buyers' minds.

- **Focus.** Your blog posts should be focused on a single topic that can then be categorized for easy website searches and SEO. A good plan is to look at your product and service list, then write blog posts on a rotating schedule, finding topics that relate to each.

Thankfully not every blog post needs to be a full article. By focusing your topic, you can create short but punchy posts that buyers enjoy. Including photos, videos, and graphics can further enhance buyer experience. Links and share buttons will help your posts find exposure in social media, and by blogging regularly, you'll find yourself with more than enough content to flesh out newsletters, emails, and social media posts, driving traffic back to your website. Furthermore, blog posts are an excellent way to draw people into newsletter sign-up and opt-in mailing lists, as long as you can deliver on your promised posting frequency.

Blogs may include a comments option, allowing buyers the chance to write responses or reviews at the bottom of each post. Whether you decide to include a comments option or not is up to you; however, you should always curate the comments lest spammers or 'negative for negative's sake' posters ruin your hard work. Many blogs require comment approval before they show up on the post itself, which I think is a good practice. Do your best to respond to and answer any comments professionally, avoiding fights or online arguments.

You may find yourself approached by other professionals who would like to guest blog on your site, especially if you've achieved high visibility or industry respect. Whether or not you decide to take this professional up on the offer will depend on who is asking, what topic they wish to post, and whether you'll have a chance to review (and possibly veto) the post before publication. Be careful about who you let post on your blog as that person's words and reputation will be attached to your business moving forward.

Articles

Articles, particularly articles published by major media outlets in print or on the web, can be a tremendous boon to your business's image as an industry expert. More of a hybrid between marketing and public relations, articles can be solicited by your contacting a publication directly or from a journalist or media contacting you after seeing your efforts elsewhere (a blog, social media). Articles attach instant credibility as buyers see that a media outlet believed you to be an expert on the article's topic. For this reason, they're also wonderful marketing tools.

Writing articles has several marketing advantages:

- **Reach.** An article is an opportunity to present your business as an expert to a fresh and new buying audience.

- **Exposure.** Even buyers familiar with your brand may not have a full grasp of what your business offers. An article that, however subtly, relates to a new or overlooked product or service can help promote it and expand your brand.

- **Lead Generating.** It's not uncommon for article writers to receive calls for help that result in new business.

Articles are similar in approach to blog writing, but with the media outlet's, not necessarily your business's, reader profile in mind. Before agreeing to an article, ask the media outlet for its most current reader profile and distribution numbers so that you can assess fit. A reader profile will help you address the proper audience while writing. You should adopt a more scholarly or educational voice with articles and avoid obvious sales pitches that the media outlet will probably (and rightfully) remove anyway. Choose a topic that's in keeping with your product or services and do your best to incorporate at least a little of your brand's style into the copy.

If you're supplying an article to a true media outlet rather than an online article collection site (such as www.ezine.com), you'll be provided with an article length in terms of word count. You may have to negotiate the title and topic, but otherwise, the article, at least in its original version, is yours to structure. You may be asked for photos or supplemental graphics for inclusion in the final article as well as a biography and head shot. Make sure to include a one to two line business profile and your website's link. Ask ahead of time about the media outlet's editing process and if you can review the final version for accuracy before it goes to press. Sometimes not, and you'll have to decide if it's worth the risk of having your name attached to a piece that might have been changed.

Journalists may want to interview you rather than have your write an article yourself. Conduct research on the journalist and read her past articles. If she seems fair and her business-related articles positive, it could be worth the risk. Always research before saying yes!

Once you're published, promote your article via social media and your business's website. If it's a printed article, ask if they offer author's copies or nice tear sheets.

Blog Radio And Podcasts

Blog radio and podcasts take blogging to another level through live or pre-recorded shows. Although a time and resource commitment, setting up your own blog radio show can be an excellent way to raise your business's profile and establish yourself as an industry expert, especially if writing isn't your strength. Blog radio is an excellent way to develop and strengthen relationships with other professionals you bring in as guests who could then refer buyers to your radio show and business. Journalists searching for industry experts look favorably upon a business with a thriving radio show and may call upon you to contribute to their own media efforts. If your radio show becomes popular, it has the potential to become a revenue stream unto itself through advertisers and sponsors.

Blog radio can have an

important impact on your marketing program, especially in terms of reach and profile. Because blog radio is digitally recorded and distributed via the web and in app stores, it's a fantastic tool for extending your business's geographic reach worldwide. If your goal is to expand your business throughout the United States, for example, bringing in experts from various parts of the country as guests can help promote your brand to their loyal buyers and cement your business as an associated expert in a new market.

Blog radio follows the same fundamental rules as blogging; your shows should offer value, relate to your business, be timely and focused. You should develop an overall show theme and maintain a consistent show schedule that buyers can rely upon. You won't need much more than a computer and a recording device as there are a number of blog radio services that can help you produce and distribute your show, including BlogTalkRadio, WSRadio, and Ubroadcast.

Mobile Apps

Mobile applications, or apps, are software created solely for use on smart phones and tablets. They take many forms: information resources, account access portals, communication mechanisms, and entertainment sources. For many businesses, they are still unchartered marketing territory. Mobile apps are often compared to websites years ago in terms of their slow but increasing importance within the business world. As more and more people incorporate smart phones and tablets into their lives, the role and relevancy of mobile apps increases.

Bloomua / Shutterstock.com

Apps can contribute to marketing in a number of ways:

- **Tracking.** Apps offer your business the opportunity to literally track your buyers and

Apps can be made available through links on your website or in app stores.

send special offers and notifications based on their geographic location, business visits, and app usage.

- **Research.** Much like other analytics tools, apps can pull buyer information based on app navigation, in-person business navigation, app-based purchase patterns, etc.

- **Shopping.** By simplifying the shopping process through online stores with stored buyer data (such as with Amazon.com's Buy Now with one click), offering easy information gathering as in the case of 'show rooming' (using smart phones to compare product or service information online while in a brick and mortar business), or targeting deals based on past shopping patterns, marketing through apps can directly contribute to your business's sales.

When properly crafted, mobile apps offer businesses branding opportunities, a value path to buyers, and enhanced customer loyalty. Why isn't every business creating an app? A challenge with mobile apps is in creating a genuine reason for your buyers to use it in the first place. Developing an app can be an expensive undertaking, and it stands to reason that your business would want some sort of return on this hefty investment. Quickly pushed, weak, or poorly constructed apps have a negative impact on buyers who may end up associating frustration or disappointment with your business itself.

As with anything else in marketing, an app has to make sense with your business and buyers. For an app to be effective, it has to offer a good reason for her to download and install it on her device. Therefore, questions to ask yourself and research before investing in an app:

- How will the app solve my buyers' needs? Is this solution of value to my buyer?

- Does the app make my buyers' life, as it relates to my brand, easier?

- Will the app be different from my competitions' apps? Will it be better?

- Can my business afford technology that minimizes buyer usage frustrations?

- Can the app be used to communicate my business's information, offers, and news to my buyers?

- Will the app be a source of marketing data?

- Does my business have the resources required to make improvements and updates to the app as technology changes in the future?

Videos

More than a commercial and testimonial platform, **video** has emerged as one of the most powerful content tools available to businesses today. As more social media channels incorporate video into their feeds, and as video-based social media channels gain followers, the marketing opportunities available to businesses become almost dizzyingly attractive. Marketing departments and social media firms salivate over potential shares and the 'viralbility' of business videos.

While it's true that videos are on a seemingly never-ending rise in viewership, not every video achieves positive results. Some fall flat and are never viewed or viewed in such low numbers as to seem a pointless effort. The question is, why are some videos successful and others not? Much of it has to do with the same rule I've mentioned with other marketing activities, buyer value. Few buyers will watch a long business commercial that only brags about accomplishments and good fortune. Or a poorly shot, badly edited how-to that shows very little. Videos consume buyer time and, as such should keep the following in mind:

Story And Obvious Message. Think of your business videos in terms of Hollywood movies. Have you ever finished a movie and said, "what was the point of that?" or "that was a waste of time"? Your videos can be subject to the same critique. You must offer a compelling reason for them to first click then stick with your video. Get to the point quickly. Have a clear message. If you're shooting a how-to video, summarize the steps involved up front, then move into the how-to portion.

Quality. While you won't necessarily need a professional videographer and full shooting set to achieve video success, there are a few quality rules that you should apply each time:

- Make sure your video is well lit and the subject matter easily seen.

- Check the audio quality and make sure that everything said is easily heard and understood, with as little background noise and distractions as possible.

- Have a clean start and end with no wobbly camera or random people walking to turn off the machine. Edit out unnecessary footage.

- Choose a camera that will shoot in a high enough resolution to produce a quality final video. You always want to start with a high quality and reduce the file size for web usage later rather than start with low quality that can't be altered or improved.

Length. Buyer attention spans are short. Many buyers jump off of longer videos, often before the messaging hits its high gear. Generally speaking, the shorter your video, the higher your viewership. Of course, well produced and engaging videos are watched at almost any length. Typical online video lengths include:

- **Teasers.** :15 seconds. The point of a teaser video is to give your buyer just enough information to whet her appetite for more. It's the lure to more involved marketing messaging commonly used in social media, on your website leading to a different page, or as short advertisements on media pages.

- **Online Commercials.** :15-45 seconds. Similar to television commercials in structure and concept, online commercials can be uploaded to social media channels such as YouTube, housed on your website, or placed as advertisements within media pages.

- **Testimonials.** :60-90 seconds. Client, customer, industry or community leaders, etc. can be excellent testimonial speakers.

- **How-To's And Tutorials.** :45-90 seconds. These can be shot in one long video or broken out into shorter videos for more involved topics.

Branding. Your business videos should always incorporate your brand and a call to action. This can be accomplished with a logo introduction, subjects in business shirts or with a branded item in the frame (subtly), and a call to action on the last frame.

Once you have your videos, you'll want to upload them to your site, social media channels, and YouTube channel. Standard digital video file extensions include: .MP4, MPEG4, .WMV, .FLV, .MOV, and .AVI. (See *Need to Know: Creative Terminology*, this chapter). YouTube will convert your files to HTML5.

Webinars

Similar to blog radio, but using a visual and audio hybrid structure, **webinars** are a more personal content format that can be delivered as a solo effort or a joint presentation between experts. Whether as recorded, on-demand files, or presented live, webinars incorporate a human voice, graphics, and often a face and video, while addressing buyer needs. They're perfect for education, how-to, and training topics where the presenter answers perceived or actual questions and discusses solutions.

Webinars can use free or paid registration, and depending on the format, presenters, and topics discussed, you may decide to absorb the production cost as a marketing effort or charge a nominal amount. Regardless, attendees will have to log in to view the webinar. Registration is a data gathering gold mine because login details should only be distributed to attendees who either

RSVP or complete a registration form. Names, email, business names, phone numbers, needs are all fair game questions in exchange for your valuable webinar.

Unless your webinar is on-demand, you should have a specific presentation date and time that can be promoted throughout your marketing program. Always list a clear webinar objective with a few supplementary bullet points and a timeframe. If you plan on having a question and answer session, list that, too, as it adds to the event's value. You should include a bio on the webinar's presenter(s), highlighting her experience with the topic.

There are numerous webinar service providers, such as WebEx and GoToMeeting, that can help facilitate your event. Always test the platform well in advance and make sure your Internet connection is up to the task. You will need a meeting space free of distractions and background noises. If you plan to use video of a presenter, make sure the room's background is professional, attractive, and incorporates some form of branding. Presentations using PowerPoint or another presentation tool should use a branded template. If you show a computer desktop, clear it of files and use a branded background.

Save your short, professional sales pitch until the end or you will lose your audience right away.

Seminars

The pre-curser to webinars, **seminars** are in-person informational events delivered to a targeted buyer audience. Marketing's approach to seminars and webinars is the same, with the exception that seminars are physically delivered in person. Because you'll need to secure a room or presentation space, printed handouts, seminars, and possibly refreshments, seminars can be more expensive undertakings than their webinar cousins. It can also be more difficult to draw an audience in without a strong lure, as busy buyers weigh transportation costs and dedicated presentation time (no muting a computer to take a call, for example) into a seminar's value.

You may decide to use a seminar as a client value-add rather than as a money-making event. By offering a seminar for free or at a reduced rate, with food, you'll have a greater chance of filling chairs with valuable buyers. Your success with seminars will depend upon several things:

Topic. Choose a topic that interests your buyers. It should be educational, but not too detailed as to narrow your audience nor too basic as to turn off all but the least informed buyers.

Presenter. A buyer's decision to spend time in a seminar is often based on the knowledge level and popularity of the presenter. High profile presenters can create a strong draw to the worst of locations and weaker topics. It's more difficult to entice buyers with a junior or completely unknown presenter.

Timely Promotion. Give yourself enough time to adequately promote your seminar. You would hate to have an empty room due to nothing more than a scheduling conflict. Begin your promotions two to three months in advance of your seminar's date.

Location. Rightly or wrongly, the quality of your seminar will be associated with your location choice. This is particularly true if you plan to serve food, even 'light refreshments.' No one will waste time on a bad meal! If you choose a low-cost, dated hall with dodgy air conditioning over an elegant country club ballroom with comfortable chairs, you must set your attendee expectations low. Make sure you choose as central and easily accessed a location as possible, with plenty of parking, good food, and a clean, professional atmosphere.

Added Perks. It's a nice touch to give your buyers something in exchange for their time. Yes, you're offering them valuable information, but that's often an overlooked point. Exclusive deals, sneak peeks, gifts, passes to future events, etc. are all nice touches that will build your seminar numbers over time.

Public Relations

Public relations, or PR, has been a workhorse in the marketing world since news began. Businesses have always angled for positive media coverage because the all important news story can trump paid advertising in a buyer's mind. There's an inherent trust between buyers and media that PR can use to your business's advantage. Traditional media, and now bloggers, rely on press releases to help fill publications by providing story ideas, quotes, facts, and community information. Bear in mind that journalists are inundated with PR requests each day, and not every release will make it to final publication or airing.

Writing A Press Release

Focused on newsworthy topics and written in a universally accepted format, **press releases** are the standard PR communication vehicle. Sent to media outlets and specific contacts, press releases are a request for press coverage. Your releases should be sent to reporters or media outlets that match with your buyer profiles. It's best to research and create a targeted list, with names and contact information, ahead of your press release's date. Otherwise, you'll not only waste your effort, but run the risk of annoying that contact for the future.

Press releases follow a style and format that isn't used elsewhere in marketing. The writing style is news-based and your releases should avoid any fluffy or back-patting language. Before writing a press release, you must first determine its news focus. Why are you sending it out? What's newsworthy about your topic? Your goal is to write more of a news story, including the 5 W's (who, what, why, when, where) and H (how) that can be easily converted into a news piece within your targeted media.

Your press release must follow the industry-wide acceptable structure. Strive to keep your press release short but informative and compelling, usually less than one page, and typed in double-spaced lines. If you have one or two quality photographs, include them with your release.

Typical Press Release Layout

Logo or Letterhead

CONTACT
Contact Name
Office phone: 111.222.1234
Cell phone: 111.222.5678
contact@emailaddress.com

FOR IMMEDIATE RELEASE: Month, Day, Year

COMPELLING HEADLINE THAT PROVIDES WHO, WHAT, WHERE, WHEN TYPE DETAILS
Subheadline that provides additional, supportive information

City, State: *Intro paragraph provides 5 W's and H in short, journalistic style copy.* Udipsuntium cus ut quatur molori doluptat rehendic tempor acepudi pitiberum est elibus, odiandis auditat ecatibus exceperum il magnim nestiae consequo velias eos alibus ma que comnis autem faccus sint dolorporum, omniet, id que ommo voluptaquis experovit faccum lit, cus.

Supporting copy provides additional information. Et aut ut venempo ribust volupta velit ut es et vendam, omnimodit dolupta tessit, net qui sa con rehent offictur sit di sim quiatur sitiist, aut aut atem de voluptaeces quiaestore es rectur autem errovide nemolupiet apictatem vendele ndelitis quamus, nim atem quia doluptiis apic te nisci sition natibus sinciis.

Include a quote from a senior executive. "Ullitis elitam ipsum hillamendis accupit, quunt pratum sit occulli cipsunt intiis unt velenda volorae volorei caborati occus et maximinim fuga. Aximus expliquam inciae quam aut descias perunte doluptaquam harundi volorernam, quiae cus ut fuga."

Il magnam et harum alitae lab is dernaturis imiliquas alit ulpa idebite mporemolest ommo doluptaessit incid quae sunt, sequibusto veni ape niaecus et molupta sincto dolendis rem conserum idi utem sum apidis reicatem aut odi con re volupta nimodiciur, necabore qui ommodit dolupta quuntius, nempos exere nisci doloreptaque volupit eturepr eremquid qui accus

Call to action (if applicable) Fugiam utempor as voleste mperia quatum quias enis nonsequ

Company bio information. Viditiandis ea qui voluptas commos ressitat lab isciis est offic tenimusda nonsequo dolupta tiamus aut quia ius estio.

###

For more information or images: Contact name and information

Release Date. Specify if this is for immediate release (the most common) or a future date (called embargo).

Headline. Your headline should be short, catchy, and with enough fact-based information to grab attention (no, "the best business in the world releases yet another winner" type headlines). This is the make or break part of a press release—it has to be good. Try to keep your headlines to less than 100 characters if you'd like journalists to use it as a social media tweet or post. You may list story-relevant hashtags, if appropriate.

Dateline. City, state of the event or where your business's news occurred.

Body Information. Start off with a news-like lead paragraph that includes your 5Ws and H in a compelling, but not sales style. Follow with two to three supporting paragraphs that are short and to the point, using facts, not fluff. Include a quote from a senior executive or person important to the event.

Contact Information. Write "for more information" in all capital letters, followed by your contact name, phone number, email address.

Business Summary. Include a brief description of your business with your URL.

End. Use "###" at the end. It is the industry accepted signal that you've concluded your release.

Sponsorships

Sponsorships are included in PR because they are generally a goodwill and supportive effort rather than a business-generating marketing tool. Unless the sponsorship comes with additional perks like an event display table, a prime opportunity to directly speak with a targeted audience, or the ability to put your product or service in front of buyers, you shouldn't expect much marketing ROI. Sponsorships are an important part of business, but

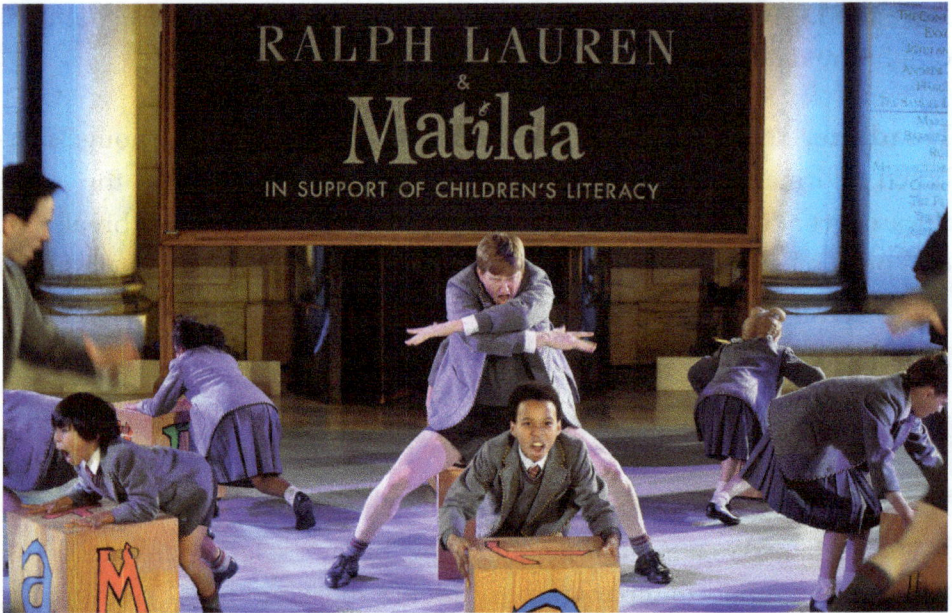

Ralph Lauren's sponsorship in Matilda supported children's literacy work.

set your expectations low on gaining buyers from your logo on a banner or in an event book.

Earned Media

Unlike owned and paid media, **earned media** doesn't link directly to your marketing budget. It's word of mouth publicity that's a by-product of your business's marketing and business practice efforts. A business referral, the sharing of a marketing piece like a web site or brochure, or non-PR instigated mention in a media setting are all considered word of mouth, and earned. Earned media can be the most lucrative form of marketing that is often a by-product of many other efforts. Achieving referral and five star reviews are a reward after your many other business investments. Thinking of it another way, your paid and owned media efforts are rewarded by earned media.

Social media and online reviews are the most visible forms of earned media. Each time your business receives a positive referral in social media or someone comments favorably on your posts, it's earned. You may not always know about earned media, especially if it's a word of mouth discussion held outside your business's control, making earned media at times difficult to track. Your best opportunities are on social media when your channel is linked, when a lead lets you know she's a referral, and, of course, online reviews.

Online Reviews

Believe it or not, your business is responsible for starting its own **online review program** and managing its online reputation. Yes, it's earned media, but without a home, your five star reviews will exist only in your buyers' minds. Creating an online review program isn't difficult and should be viewed as an important branding step that ensures a consistent message. It can also drive traffic to your website and social media pages, which, in turn, could have a positive SEO impact. Establishing a program will help ensure that you have the resources set aside to monitor and report results.

Using review sites can be a tremendous asset to your business, as both a buyer influencer and marketing research tool. Maintaining high ratings can be looked at as an exercise in quality and customer service control, and even be a form of brand penetration if you read through buyer comments on your products or services. Keep in mind that negative reviews happen and that there's little to be gained by starting an online war. Answer any direct comments professionally and as helpfully as possible, and save the battles for another day.

Industry Review Sites

Your first step is to create pages on key review sites, such as your industry specific sites, or on more global review websites like Yelp.com, and Google+ Local. Your business and buyer types will determine your exact review mix. For example, a travel-based business may be best suited for a site such as TripAdvisor.com, while a restaurant may want to pursue a profile on UrbanSpoon.com or OpenTable.com. A selection of the more universal ratings sites includes:

Yelp.com. Under fire for some of its review manipulation and 'advertise to improve rankings' practices, Yelp.com is still a buyer information source and worth setting up a profile, especially if yours is a BtoC business. Known as 'claiming,' setting up your own Yelp business profile will help you control overall business information, including your service list, website, contact information, etc. Reviewers can type a message and rank your business on a one to five star scale. It's free to buyers.

Google+ Local. A part of Google, Google+ Local is a powerful review tool that connects directly with Google's local search engine results. Businesses must qualify as a Google+ Local page through direct, in-person interactions at a verifiable address (no remote locations or call centers) and the use of straight-forward taglines free from sales influencers. It is an ideal local buyer resource. Creating a presence starts with establishing a Google Places for Business page, then creating a Google+ Local page. It also uses a one to five star rating scale. Free to buyers.

Yahoo Local. Similar in style and intent to Google+ Local, Yahoo Local is connected to its Yahoo search engine. Buyers can search by name, category, or business type. It uses a one to five star rating scale and is free to buyers.

Local.com. Set up as a directory site, Local.com allows buyers to search by name, category, or business type and displays results in a directory type list. It does offer paid premium listings and uses a one to five star rating scale. Free to buyers.

Angie's List. A subscription-based review site, Angie's List allows members to see more in-depth reviews and special discounts. It's designed as a business rating tool with member input developing the overall letter-based rating (A is the highest). Paid membership.

Website & Social Media

The second step in your online review program is setting up a review and testimonial capture system on your website and social media pages. This could be as simple as adding ratings to a product page or enabling reviews on Facebook, depending on what your business has in place online. The goal is to make it easy for buyers to submit a review. You should have an easy system by which spam reviews can be removed. As long as you avoid becoming obnoxious or spammy, you may solicit reviews and testimonials. Testimonial requests should be made personally, especially if the testimonial format is longer than a written line or two. You may incorporate reviews from other sites into your own website, especially if you have high reviews and are marketing locally.

Shopping sites. Shopping sites like Amazon.com employ a robust buyer review system that you can use if you have products sold on that site. While your business can't (ethically) control the reviews on an outside shopping site, you can create a business page within that site and include more information about your products and business approach.

Business Review Services. Don't overlook the advantages to reviews and listings within sites such as the Better Business Bureau (BBB), Consumer Reports, or J.D. Power & Associates. Yes, securing a review per these business's standards will require work; however, the resulting accreditation and bragging rights can be well worth the effort.

Trade Shows & Events

At some point in your business life cycle you may contemplate exhibiting at a **trade show** or **special event**. Trade shows differ from other marketing activities in that they include an element of personal sales in addition to the basic marketing rules. This crazy, hectic part of marketing often means long hours, significant investments, and confusing, paperwork-driven details completely foreign to the average person.

In-person events can be an outstanding way to present a business to a captive, often highly targeted buying audience. Understanding what you're getting into will prepare you for the chaos and prevent budget-busting penalties and add-ons late in the process.

Picking The Right Show

There's no getting around the fact that trade shows and events are an expensive investment, with some costing well into the hundreds of thousands of dollars. While most smaller businesses won't need to spend a fraction of that amount, when you factor in the cost of displays, collateral, the space itself, and staffing your booth, no event will be an insignificant investment. This is why the first step is determining whether or not a show is truly right for your business. Things to check before signing up include:

Attendance Numbers. No matter how fantastic your booth space, congestion, traffic flow, outside distractions, educational sessions, and networking periods will mean that you will only speak with a (small) portion of any event's attendees. Ask yourself, will the event offer enough traffic to make the show worth my while?

Other Exhibitors. Will the exhibitor mix draw enough of your targeted buyers? How many of your competitors will exhibit? How many total exhibitors will be in the hall(s)? Too few and attendees may skip over the hall; too many and it could be difficult to stand out.

Show Draws. Are the speakers and break-out sessions enough to draw your target buyers? This is of particular importance with larger, destination type shows that can be expensive. If the draw isn't strong enough, buyers won't waste their travel budget.

Show Hours. When is the exhibit hall open? Is it open long enough to warrant your time and money? Will the hall be open at the right times, allowing for meaningful sales conversations (i.e., not just first thing or at the end of the day)?

Extra Costs. Depending on where the event is held, you may face extra costs such as union fees, electricity charges, maid services, furniture rentals, plants, on-site storage, in-show deliveries, badge fees, etc. These charges can accumulate quickly and push the cost of the event out of your budget's reach. The key to surviving this money pit unscathed is carefully reading all paperwork ahead of time, adhering to the show's rules, and meeting the early bird rate deadlines. Creating a show book or file with all forms and dates organized by deadline will help keep you on track.

Setting Up A Booth Space

Once you've determined a show is a match with your business, the next step is choosing and setting up your exhibit space. Event spaces can vary, depending on the show type and venue hall itself. Most smaller businesses end up with the standard 10 foot x 10 foot or 10 foot x 20 foot space; however, there are times when exhibiting at shows with five foot draped tables set end to end makes sense. Larger businesses may opt for larger spaces that require significantly more planning and work, including hiring installation and construction teams. Regardless of the type, there are a few trade show basics associated with setting up any event space:

Placement. The name of the game with any event is catching attendees' attention quickly, meaning that choosing the right space will make or break your ROI. Few businesses have a profitable show when stuck in the dark corner of an annex hall. Look at the show's exhibit map and pick a place that has good traffic and allows you to show off your business to its best advantage. In general, it's a good practice to pick the place yourself rather than leaving it up to the event's staff as they're often more interested in filling a show hall than selling your business. Corner spaces offer a dual traffic advantage and increased layout options.

Clear Message. Always keep your booth simple, on brand, and easily understood. Gimmicky set-ups can pull people in; however, the gimmick has to be quickly grasped, and, most important, in keeping with your products or services. If an attendee has to pause and really study your booth to understand it, your set-up is too complicated!

Professional Design Counts. A trade show booth is a reflection of your business itself, and amateur design can look "mom and pop" next to a professional's cleanly branded work. An amateur booth setup will make your business seem small and insignificant in attendees' eyes and encourage them to walk past without stopping. With all the money spent on securing a space, staffing the booth, and even travel, it's a shame to lose business due to poorly designed graphics and collateral. Do yourself a favor and hire a professional!

Keep It Clean. An open, clutter-free layout is inviting and will help quickly deliver your business message. Clean, professional signage and uncluttered display layouts will allow visitors to review your product or service, and engage immediately. Fewer displayed products are more effective as sales tools than throwing every option onto a cluttered table. Measure your furniture and make sure it's not too big or bulky for your space. Keeping the booth clean also applies to housekeeping. A tidy space is inviting, a dirty space is not. Hide your boxes and throw out your trash!

Product Front And Center. Most show attendees are reluctant to stop and walk into a booth space, meaning that if all of your product or service information is in the back of your booth or cluttered on a table with you standing in front, you're exhibiting with a handicap. Keep a few teaser products at the very front of a booth on a high counter as quick conversation starters. Stand and smile from behind the counter; you'll have an easier time catching a passing attendees's attention with, "have you seen x product?" Never turn your back to the show floor!

Videos And Interactive Displays. These can be powerful tools, as long as they don't compete with your business's message. With smaller booths, placing videos on display tables at the sides of the booth will leave the center open for your logo, message, samples, and staff. In larger booths, pillars and walls are excellent video spots.

Light It Up. Dark booths don't sell! Invest in multiple light options and light your booth up!

Working Your Booth

The booth's setup is only half of your process; next you'll need to properly staff the booth. It's a good practice to have your staff plan on spending more time than expected at the show and in the set-up / break-down process. It always takes longer than expected!

Standing vs. Sitting. My rule is to never sit in the booth while attendees are on the floor. It may sound brutal, but the booth is there to generate business, and nothing makes attendees walk past a space faster than a booth worker sitting down. If you don't have the energy to stand and sell, why should your buyers (who have been walking on painful floors), stop and talk? The one exception to the "not sitting down" rule is to perch / lean on a hidden stool concealed behind a counter set at the front of the booth.

Wardrobe. Always wear comfortable dress shoes, even if you've sprung for extra carpet padding. You're going to be on your feet all day! Make sure your outfit is approachable, professional, ready for work (such as moving collateral boxes or samples), and just a little more formal than what attendees are wearing. You won't want to make a casually dressed attendee uncomfortable while standing next to you in a formal suit or outlandish outfit. If your goal is to gain business, leave the sexy clothes at home—you'll attract the wrong attendees and may miss real opportunities.

peruciatti / Shutterstock.com

Trade shows involve long, hectic days spent trying to catch attendees' attention.

Be Warm And Engaging. Smile and speak with everyone, including your fellow exhibitors! Business and referrals can come from all types of people at an event.

Empty Booth. Empty booths can mean lost opportunities and should be avoided as much as possible. Restroom breaks are a human requirement, but if it's your time to work the booth, try to have someone else cover you while you quickly take a break. Bringing bottled water and snacks that can be discreetly consumed will help you stay energized without having to leave your booth to fend for itself.

Trade Show Etiquette

Etiquette is an often overlooked but oh-so-important part of the event world. Some of your best business deals may come from fellow exhibitors later in a show who may hire your business directly or refer you to friends. Knowing this, it's always a smart policy to be respectful and helpful to your fellow exhibitors. My no-no's include:

Don't Interrupt Traffic Flow. Standing in front of your fellow exhibitors' booths and / or blocking their traffic flow is a no-no. An example is a next-door neighbor standing on the edge of the booth space or to the side of a table with a group of people, forcing traffic to by-pass your own booth. That's potentially lost business, and it's uncool when they do it. Don't do it yourself.

Don't Visually Block. Blocking your fellow exhibitors with signs, plants, graphics, or other obstructions is insensitive and rude. Larger shows may have a 4' rule, meaning that nothing taller than 3-4' can be placed greater than 4' from the back of the space. It's a good practice to make sure the hall's visual lines are free for everyone.

Avoid Nuisance Marketing. One of my biggest exhibitor pet peeves relates to exhibitors who pollute the hall with music, videos with sound, scent-based displays, smoke machines, flashy lights, or anything that's distracting and inescapable by your fellow exhibitors. Just don't do it.

Set-Up Late / Break-Down Early. Be mindful of the show's hours and make sure your booth is set-up and ready for visitors during the show hours. My rule of thumb is breakdown doesn't occur until the floor is cleared of visitors, and I've made many a deal from attendees wandering the halls after my fellow exhibitors have broken down. *Never* break down early. Many shows levy penalties on exhibitors inconsiderate enough to break down early, for good reason. Empty spaces create a negative atmosphere over everyone else still on the floor.

Sales Packages / RFI / RFP

Although the two are separate departments, marketing is often pulled into the world of sales through the creation of **sales packages**, **Request for Proposals (RFP)**, or **Request for Informations (RFI)** bid packages. This is because marketing is the keeper of the business story, and generally has writers with content that can be modified and approved brand graphics at the ready.

Depending on what entity made the initial request, there may be rules or layout requirements that must be followed if the bid is to be granted consideration. This is especially true with government entities that may dictate page structure down to approved graphic formats and the font and size used. These requirements can be so strict that larger businesses create separate teams staffed with expert bid designers and writers. Smaller businesses may have to use whatever marketing resources can be mustered up and should allow ample learning-curve and proofing time to make sure what's sent checks all the required boxes.

If bid packages are a routine occurrence in your business, it's worth investing the time to create approved boilerplate that answers common questions. Time should be spent researching all requirements well before the bid's due date. This won't negate the need for subject matter expert input on answering questions, but can prevent too many late-night editing rounds hours before the bid package's deadline. Bid packages always take longer than expected, and it's in your business's best interest to begin work as early as possible.

Need To Know: Design Basics

While this book isn't intended as a design book, there are basic guidelines of design that will help keep your projects on track:

- Never use more than one to two, possibly three fonts in a design, including all caps and all lowercase within the same font family. Too many different types of fonts makes a design look busy. Your logo may count toward your font number if it's text based.

- Use white (blank) space to your advantage. It will give your buyers an eye rest and allow the focus to stay on important details.

- Clutter is your enemy! Keep your design and message clean and easily read.

- Never bury your message and logo. They should be easily spotted. Usually the headline is your primary focal point and the logo your anchor.

- Don't put important information on trim lines or creases.

- Short, punchy lines or lists are better than heavy text no one will read.

- A strong single graphic can speak more loudly than many smaller ones.

- Small lines of text can be difficult for many buyers to read.

- Be mindful of the design's end use. Heavy color may not translate well in newsprint while black and white may not be as effective in digital. Keep in mind the quality of printing presses you will use in print. If they're sub-par, you won't want to use a heavily detailed design.

5. I Think I Can Set A Marketing Budget

Why Do You Need A Budget?

What every business owner eventually realizes, sometimes too late, is that business can't exist without marketing generated awareness. And without awareness, you'll realize few to no sales. Therefore, no matter your business's size, money must be spent on marketing. Money, in this case, can take form in hard currency or in time and labor.

This is why one of my first questions to any new client who asks about marketing options is, "what is your budget?" Often this question is followed by a surprised look and perhaps some hemming and hawing with a long, "welllll. . ." The next words are usually, "how much *should* I spend?" While I'm more than happy to suggest a budget to any client, only she knows what her business can comfortably support.

By taking the time to set aside a marketing budget, you'll be able to prioritze opportunities identified in your marketing strategy and move forward with a solid plan of action based on real marketplace data and project costs. Surprises do happen, but having a budget will help keep your marketing program on track and in front of the right buyers.

Setting Your Marketing Budget

Setting your **marketing budget** is one of the trickiest parts of business management. It's also one of the most important. Set aside too little and it could mean a loss in sales. Set aside too much and it could mean another aspect of your business will have to be cut to cover the difference. Set no budget at all and you could quickly face a pile of marketing invoices that eat at money reserves meant to last all year.

The biggest barrier to setting a marketing budget is overcoming the fear associated with spending your hard-won dollars. This fear exists because there is no absolute guarantee that a marketing campaign will create an overnight success out of your business, and it's tough to spend money on a gamble. It would be easier with a surefire formula of $1 in marketing = $5 in sales, but that formula simply can't exist. Variations in target audiences, marketplaces, buying seasons, economic influences, current brand awareness, and expenses within the marketing tools themselves combined make it impossible to create such a formula. The closest thing you'll have to a crystal ball is your marketing strategy, which is designed to allow for more risk as your business grows.

So how much should you spend on marketing each year? The answer to that question largely depends on where your business is in its life cycle, its size, and the industry within which you're marketing combined with your resources and goals. Questions to ask yourself include:

- How much buyer awareness and marketing infrastructure do I have in place? Will any of it need to be updated or replaced this year?

- Am I looking to expand into a new market(s) or target a new buyer? If so, how far away are they from my current market? Is there buyer overlap or will my brand have to start from scratch?

- Am I introducing new products or services?

- Will I have additional packaging, point of sale, or other product-related marketing needs?

- Am I planning a complete re-brand?

As a general rule, the earlier your business is in its growth, as in the case of startups, the more money you'll need to allocate. Product-based businesses generally have higher marketing needs than service-based. Typical annual budget ranges by business size are:

Startups to One year: 10-20%

New businesses need an entire marketing program from scratch, including higher dollar projects like a marketing strategy, full branding program, and a website. Some of these items are one time, or once in a few year expenses, and should be looked upon as foundation projects in your marketing infrastructure. Other expenses such as campaigns and advertising increase brand awareness and are treated as recurring expenses.

Established businesses with limited expansion, Large, 3-5%

Large businesses can get away with spending a lower percentage of revenue simply because they bring in more money. Your marketing infrastructure is in place, and most of your budget is allocated to awareness and buyer engagement efforts.

Established businesses with limited expansion, Small, 5-7%

Smaller businesses bring in less revenue, requiring a higher percentage allocated to marketing just to cover costs. Like larger businesses, much of your marketing infrastructure should be in place, with awareness and buyer engagement as your major marketing expenses.

Established businesses, complete re-branding, 7-15%

Unless your business is on the extreme ends of the business size scale, expect to spend 7-15% on a complete re-brand. You are essentially starting over at this stage. Your marketing infrastructure will have to be overhauled or replaced, and a new marketing strategy and branding program introduced business-wide.

Established businesses, completely new market, 5-15%

Businesses targeting a completely new market will have to invest more heavily to generate brand awareness. The farther the new market is from your current market, the more you may have to rely on transportation costs, marketing modifications (what works in your current market, may not work in the new market), and awareness campaigns.

Steps To Developing Your Budget

Step 1 in setting a budget with a chance at a return involves understanding how your business fits within your chosen marketplace and who you're trying to attract as a buyer. In other words, the first step is reviewing your marketing strategy and comparing its activities with your current resources and calendar.

Step 2 involves calculating all the costs associated with the marketing strategy's activities, priority or not. This is a tricky part of the budget process because most projects have multiple costs associated with their development and execution. A trade show, for example, could have many line items beyond a booth space registration, and a business will need to budget for each step or face a nasty financial surprise. Working through your list, put as many real numbers next to projects as possible, taking the extra steps to call media outlets and ask for rate cards and price out projects internally or through outsourced suppliers. You may choose to use ballpark numbers for projects that may change in a few months.

It's tempting to look for ways to cut corners in Step 2, but sacrificing quality to save budget is risky. There are times when choosing a lower priced project makes sense, but keep in mind that making purchases or hiring outside resources solely based on price could end up costing you more in the long run. An excellent example is launching a cheap, templated website rather than spending a little more for a custom site that truly sells your business and is built using modern technology. Sure, you'll save money for the short-term, but the project will have to be re-worked and replaced in the near future, compounding the original project's price.

Once your business has a clear picture of its buyer, marketplace, and the costs associated with your planned marketing activities, you can then move to **Step 3,** comparing the results with your business's financials and other planned expenditures. Historic business data is tremendously helpful during this step, and comparing your marketing calendar concept with your business's revenue cycle will help you forecast your budgeting needs. If, for example, your marketing strategy suggests performing a high priority project during a traditionally low-revenue time of the year, you'll need to budget in advance.

Step 4 is simply writing out the budget's line items by calendar timeline and frequency. Typically this is done both monthly and quarterly and lists each activity as its own line item. For projects that run more than once, total each project by your frequency allocation, say monthly, and again as an annual total. Match those totals against your comfortable spend number and see how they compare. If you're high, look at your calendar, project by project, and cut wish list or non-priority items. Of course, review your spend number and make sure it's not too conservative to achieve your goals.

You'll want to revisit your budget after each quarter to determine project effectiveness. Obviously some projects will take longer to show ROI, but others like PPC campaigns should give you a sense of their returns fairly soon after launch.

Pricing Your Projects

I wish I could write down a list of prices for the most common projects encountered in marketing, but variances within market and firm pricing and the deliverables you'll receive make such a list difficult. For example, I'd expect a large marketing firm in Manhattan servicing Fortune 100 companies to charge more than one in a small USA town servicing small businesses. It's true that price isn't always an indicator of value, but it is of markets and clientele.

Suffice it to say, bigger projects are going to cost more, and if the price you're quoted seems to good to be true, it probably is. You shouldn't expect grand results from a marketing strategy that costs you a few hundred dollars and is only a few pages long, nor should you pay tens of thousands for a simple landing page.

Seminars can lead to new business and buy-in if they're properly organized and promoted. If not, they're nothing more than wasted budget.

As a rule of thumb, marketing strategies and full branding programs start in the thousands of dollars and, depending on your market, size of business, deliverable type, and your consulting firm itself, could run into the tens to hundreds of thousands of dollars. Web sites are in the same range and are dependent upon your site requirements. Most other projects are less. Obviously only the largest businesses need projects at the upper ends of those ranges and smaller businesses at the lower. The trade off in price is the value you'll receive from an experienced firm who will put the necessary time and effort toward your success.

If you're unsure of your market's pricing, contact a few consultants and request ballpark prices for your specific projects using the advice in Chapter 6. Always be courteous and up front about your stage in the project and share that you're contacting other firms.

Ways To Waste Money In Marketing

Part of your budget development process should include cutting or eliminating projects with zero to low ROI. These projects may have been inherited from a previous owner or manager or existed before your marketing strategy and now have no place in your new, enlightened program.

Once you start looking at projects in closer detail you'll see that ROI challenges start behind the scenes, before budget dollars are spent. The following are a few of the more common ways to waste money in marketing.

Taking On Too Broad A Buying Audience

As we discussed in Chapter 2, to be successful in marketing, you need to identify and understand your buying audience and communicate your brand message accordingly. This is even more true in marketing where a company's message is communicated on a mass scale rather than the easily adapted face-to-face sales environment. Mistakenly embracing an 'all things to all people' approach will fail. Your marketing will have to carry either a flat, generic message that won't motivate anyone or produce a vast collection of marketing materials addressing individual buyer types. Referred to as, "shotgun marketing," the only way to make this approach work is to have an unlimited marketing budget and a team of marketers to customize an infinite number of communications. The better solution is to allocate a little budget toward profiling your business's true buyer(s), which will ultimately save money and yield positive results.

Skipping Due Diligence

Not every marketing opportunity that comes your way will have been identified in your original marketing strategy. That doesn't mean you should pull the trigger without first performing due diligence. No opportunity is so urgent that you can't take a moment to perform research, even if that's limited to a quick web search. Sales executives are notorious for calling with deals and specials that require immediate responses—don't give in to the pitch! Review your numbers, investigate the opportunity, and make a decision based on best fits with your marketing program and budget.

Nixing Your Marketing Budget

When times are tough, pulling back on marketing may seem like a responsible business decision, but cutting marketing will only end up costing you business, compounding your business woes. Marketing is the path by which new buyers are discovered and become engaged in the business's products or services, which means that, without marketing, your chances of securing new buyers and their life sustaining revenue dollars dramatically diminish. Rather than nixing marketing outright, it's better to scale back and focus on core or priority efforts that will provide the biggest bang for your buck.

If research shows a marketing effort is a good match with your business's targeted buyers, consistency is required to have any kind of impact. As frustrating as it might be to wait, it takes time to build buyer loyalty and convince a buyer to part with her money. Too many business owners try something once, then bemoan that they didn't receive any business from the effort. Of course not! People today are inundated with advertisements and messages, and it's easy to miss a single effort. Trying a series of one-off's or spitting and spurting one's way through communications will result in spotty results and low ROI. Instead, rely on your strategy's research, narrow down the list to the best possible options. Try them at least three times.

Going Overboard On Promotional Items

It can be great fun to see your business logo and business name on *everything*, but beware that the giveaway and gimme promotional field is littered with money wasting landmines. Despite what a promotional company may pitch, businesses don't gain clients from items like pens, branded candy, koozies, stress balls, mouse pads, pocket tip cards, etc. And no one is going to cross an exhibit hall to pick up a keychain! The reality is that these items almost always end up in a junk drawer, the trash, or in a kid's toy chest, meaning that they're wasted marketing dollars.

Promotional items certainly have their place in marketing, but for them to have any value in your program, they need to be unique, truly useful in the buying audience's world, and desirable. One of my most popular gimmes was a branded, nice quality magnifying glass distributed at a technical trade show. Every attendee had a job that required reading papers and technical drawings with fine print and my booth was the hit of the show once word got out about our gimmes. Our brand was front and center at that show and the glasses stayed visible on many desks long after the show's close. The magnifying glasses were so popular that people contacted me for replacements when theirs broke years later!

In the same vein, unless your business has a knockout logo and an established brand with incredible caché, buying branded coffee mugs, t-shirts, ball caps, etc. for resale is another way to flush money down the toilet.

Opting For Cheap Now Leads To Spending More In the Future

There's a time and place for seeking out low priced options; however, when it comes to your brand and developing marketing program, sometimes paying more is the most cost-effective option. 'Cheapening out' in key marketing areas often requires expensive repairs and fixes in the not too distant future. This is especially true in higher level work where experience and expertise matter more than price. A good example is using a junior marketer or design house to create your marketing strategy, the plan that will dictate all of your marketing efforts, including your budget, and your brand's visual identity. Sure, these options may be less expensive up front, but can your business afford to follow inexperienced advice?

Another situation relates to technology and infrastructure, as in the case of business website development. Yes, there are free or inexpensive website options available, but these are often cookie cutter, functionally restricted sites that use dated or limited technology. Since the buying public is increasingly using mobile and tablet devices for web browsing, that inexpensive website may cost you much more in lost business from buyers who won't deal with an outdated, cumbersome technology. Boring design and limited functionality will reflect badly on your business and can have a tremendous impact on your brand.

Overruns On Expensive Brochures & Sales Folders

As discussed in Chapter 4, collateral such as brochures and sales packages can be invaluable tools, particularly for non-retail and service-based businesses. Printing years' worth of multi-page corporate brochures and sales folders to achieve a lower per unit price; however, can be costly. Businesses should change and adapt with their marketplace, and predicting buyer trends years out is nearly impossible. You may decide to change products or cut services, add new ones, change locations, re-brand, etc, at which point the collateral on your shelf will become obsolete.

Digital printing has been perfected to the point where ganging large runs of more generic materials to keep press costs down is no longer much of an issue. In fact, affordable digital printing allows businesses to completely customize their materials and print only what they need, ensuring fresh and on-target materials—and cleaner storage rooms.

Advertising Space & Sponsorships

Sponsorships can be both business smart and socially beneficial community efforts; unfortunately, saying yes to every opportunity will rapidly eat up your marketing budget. Businesses should choose to support nonprofits and local efforts carefully. Select a few that best reflect your business's personality, beliefs, and, again, target audience. Sharing this support via your business website and social media outlets will let buyers and other sponsorship solicitors know that you care, but that your budget has been earmarked.

Re-Branding Without Cause

Re-Branding can be a healthy business response to changes within your marketplace, buyers, products or services, societal trends, or to correct a poorly developed brand. This won't change the fact that it's an expensive and disruptive process as your new brand will have to be implemented business-wide. Re-branding should never be undertaken without first running through the branding steps outlined in Chapter 3. It's important to keep your brand current and make sure it speaks to the right buyers, but only re-brand if it's absolutely necessary. Re-Branding 'just cause' to incorporate new favorite colors, a relative's interpretation of a logo, inspiration on a new name, or other such whims is a stupid waste of marketing money.

Not Following Up On Opportunities

One of the biggest ways to waste money in marketing is to focus on collecting leads without taking the extra steps to follow up on them. Outside of research, leads are absolutely useless until they're converted to sales! Following up doesn't mean having an intern send a form email or shuffling a lead from employee to employee before someone leaves a stiff and rambling voice mail weeks later. For marketing to have any value, a business must develop a lead follow-up program and stick with it every time. The business world is riddled with stories of seemingly lesser leads turned into unexpectedly big clients, and a good rule is to follow-up with each lead, just in case. Your business should never be too busy to personally follow-up on solid leads within 24-48 hours.

Hosting Open Houses & Networking Events

Hosting an open house or networking event can be an excellent way to commemorate a number of years in business, a new and exciting service or achievement, or to thank your buyers, as long as you put enough time into the planning and execution process to make it worth your while. Your dreams of using your event to build business and subtly sell to a captive audience can quickly become a costly failure when too few (if any) of the right kind of buyer show up. Why? Many times it's because the event was put together at the last minute, on a day that conflicts with another event, without a strong enough draw, or was under-promoted. If a business is going to host an event, it should take the time to plan it properly, with a theme, nice door prizes, good food, and well scheduled and timely promotions targeting prime buyers. There are few situations in marketing more frustrating than spending event money only to have a few family members and that one longtime client with nothing better to do show up.

Bundled Projects

Marketing is never a one size fits all exercise, and trying to force a marketing project bundle on a business usually results in at least one unnecessary project. It's far better to work with a firm or service provider that offers à la carte project or service pricing that can be customized for your specific business rather than spending money on something you don't need or want. That way you'll save your marketing budget for projects you actually need and can afford. It's also the best way to execute a marketing strategy's project list, particularly in terms of a timeline.

6. I Think I Can Work With Consultants & Suppliers

Eventually you'll find yourself hiring outside consultants or suppliers, the success of which will largely depend on your working relationship. Outside professionals can become a tremendous asset to your business with their ability to offer niche expertise, specific project oversight, and needed services and products. In the case of consultants, they can fill holes in your marketing program's structure and provide outside evaluation and ideas. Those who develop successful relationships with their outside team members can reap the rewards of a trusted resource who's available to help in a time of need.

The advantage to fostering a positive, productive consultant or supplier relationship doesn't rest solely on your paying the bill! True, you're paying for their work, but additionally investing in the attention and time required by your provider will help your outside projects run smoothly, stay on budget, and meet deadlines. My career has placed me on both sides of the relationship, as a client and consultant, and I've learned how to avoid the common pitfalls and keep projects moving happily forward.

Articulating Needs

While many suppliers are professionals well-versed in speaking "client," they will need at least basic information from you before they can accurately scope and price a project. The more forthcoming you are and the more requested details you share, the better the outcome. While no consultant or supplier should expect you to provide all of a project's pieces, most will need to understand the purpose of your project and how it fits within your ultimate goal.

Before contacting a consultant or supplier, take a moment to describe your need to yourself:

- Why are you contacting her?

- Is there a specific need or an overreaching goal that needs to be addressed?

- Are there any features about this project that the consultant or supplier needs to include in a pricing proposal?

- What is your timeline? Are there important deadlines that need to be met?

- What is your budget?

- Are you ready to hire today or are you on a fact-finding mission?

The best consultants and suppliers will attempt to draw this information and more out of you in the initial conversation, then again before your project kick-off. Depending on the scope and type of work, this could be conducted through a questionnaire or series of exhaustive interviews via phone, video chat, or in-person. If your consultant or supplier is a seasoned veteran, each question should be relevant and necessary, making them important to your project's process. Of course, if your consultant doesn't ask many questions or seems disinterested, you may want to shop around and find another resource.

Be prepared to answer these questions; your consultants can't work in a vacuum. Imagine if you walked into a bakery and asked for cake, but didn't share your desired size, type, flavor, or decorating theme? How will the baker know what you want? And without knowing what you want, how could the

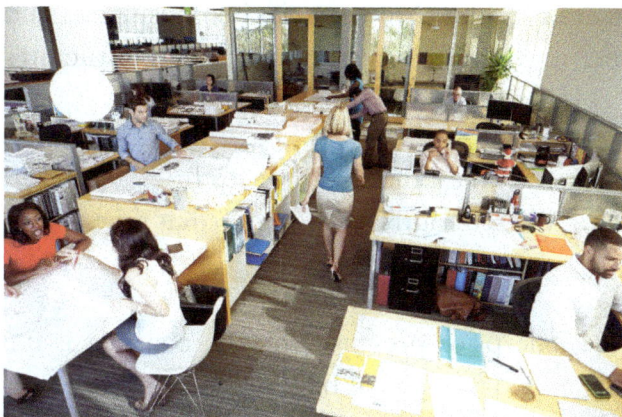

baker possibly give you a price? She can't.

Help your consultant or supplier out by answering questions thoroughly. Skipping questions, providing vague or brief answers, or leaving information out will only hurt your project and make the entire process more difficult.

You don't have to share your entire marketing budget's number in a pre-contract conversation, but you should have a dollar amount in mind to prevent wasting an out-priced consultant or supplier's time. You should also be a little further down the path than "what if" before fully engaging a consultant or supplier. If you're performing a price check, be fair and ask for ballpark numbers rather than request a detailed (and labor intensive) proposal. It doesn't help your brand to have a reputation as a price shopper or tire kicker, and the best person for the job may not be as eager to work with you if you waste her time early on.

Read The Contract!

No matter what type of consultant or supplier you hire, the tone of your relationship begins early on, before you make your first payment. You both must first understand, and agree to, the terms and scope of your project. In other words, read the contract before signing.

Each consultant or supplier will have her own process for kicking-off your new project. Some will start with an abbreviated proposal followed by an in-depth contract while others will have a simple order form attached to a terms and conditions requirement. All should have a description of the project's deliverable, payment terms, a timeframe, and what you'll need to provide during the project's creation. More corporate consultants and suppliers will include terms and conditions. Typical pricing structures include:

- **Hourly rates:** You'll be given an estimate of time up front and billed for time actually worked at the set hourly rate, even if that time is over the original estimate.

- **Project or lump sum:** The price presented on the contract is the entire price, with nothing added to the final bill.

- **Time and materials:** You will be charged for the exact time worked on your project plus any additional expenses incurred during that timeline (i.e., travel, media placement, talent hires, etc.)

Projects always run more smoothly when both client and consultant or supplier understand and adhere to the scope, deadlines, and deliverables outlined in the contract. Taking a little time to properly set both sides' expectations and understand what's listed in the project's contract before starting will help everyone involved avoid confusion and wasted effort.

Before signing a contract, both you and your consultant or supplier should be able to answer:

- What is the project deliverable exactly? Is this what I had in mind?

- What are my responsibilities in this project?

- What are the important deadlines in this project?

- What does the proofing process look like?

- How will my consultant or supplier use my project once we're finished (will it be included in a portfolio, for example)?

- What will I, the client, receive at the end of the project (i.e., file types,

PDFs, tear sheets, recordings)?

- How will I pay for this project? Is project delivery dependent upon payment(s)?

If you're unable to answer any of the above, speak with your consultant or supplier about your questions. It's important that you understand the project's process and requirements before it starts. Surprisingly, there are business owners and representatives who sign contracts without first reading and *understanding* the details! Remember, both sides will always have a role to play in your project's process, even if your own role is limited to providing files and information up front. Make sure that you can fulfill your responsibilities by the time allotted or suffer project delays, a souring relationship, and possibly financial penalties.

Communications

Once your contract has been signed and your project officially started, it's time to assume your role as a client. Have you heard that old saying, "communication is a two-way street?" This wisdom is of particular use when working with outside consultants and suppliers who don't have the luxury of catching you in the hall with questions. Nothing delays a project faster than poor communication, and having to chase down information or scheduled payments will swiftly move your project down the priority list. Consultants and suppliers work best with engaged, responsive clients who understand their role within the project. Not surprisingly, clients work best with engaged, responsive consultants and suppliers. Both sides need to be part of the project for it to succeed.

Understanding Supplier Roles

Consultants and suppliers are available for just about anything that could touch your marketing department and can be invaluable resources. They may take form as trusted advisors or go-to resources you can call on again and again. Taking a moment to understand how your consultants and supplier can benefit your business will help you decide what resources you need and where you should budget your time and money.

Industry Experts? Before diving in, I'd like to address whether or not you should hire a consultant or supplier experienced in your industry or business type. My answer is not necessarily. While experts who focus on one area will know industry players and what is accepted by the typical buyer, I've found that the marketing principals outlined in this book apply universally and an industry specialist firm is not always an advantage. In fact, specialist firms may be so tied to an industry that their projects become cookie-cutter or similar to the point where the competition blurs together.

I can think of a couple of past worked industries where the technology used was comparatively behind the times but generally accepted as 'cutting edge' within that industry. I've also experienced industry pricing, which was often above non-industry rates. While I'm not saying that industry experience should be discarded or lacks value, it shouldn't be your primary decision maker. A fresh perspective can help set your business apart!

Need To Know: Warning Signs You've Hired The Wrong Firm

I'd love to say every consultant and supplier you'll encounter will act professionally and become a valuable part of your team, but that's not a business reality. As I'll cover later on in this chapter, some relationships can sour from bad client actions while others were doomed from the start because of the consultant or supplier herself. If you've been a model client and experience any of the following, you may have hired the wrong firm:

- **Disinterest in your project, business need, or goals.** Disinterest can be tracked by a lack of questions, follow-up, or sloppy work. Usually this is an indicator early on or before a project kicks-off.

- **Unresponsive to your phone calls and emails.** People are busy and work does interfere, but if you haven't heard back from your primary contact in 24 hours (on weekdays) or on Monday after a weekend, there may be a bigger issue brewing. You definitely have a problem if no one in the firm responds.

- **Routinely breaking promises.** If your consultant or supplier says she'll have a project or proof for you by a specified deadline, then pushes the date without good reason (such as implementing your change in vision), you may have a problem on your hands.

- **Asking for more money.** Unless you've made changes to the project, she should adhere to the contract. A money request could mean problems within the firm or a lack of scheduling / forecasting experience.

- **Your contact within the firm changes repeatedly.** Unless there's been an official handoff as in the case of an account executive to a project manager, your firm should maintain a primary point of contact throughout your project. If that contact changes more than once, it may indicate bigger problems within the firm itself.

Marketing Firms

Marketing firms come in all shapes and sizes, with some focused on a specific marketing niche and others offering a more full-service, one-stop-shop approach. Your individual business needs and the health and depth of your own program will dictate who you should hire. If, for example, your business has a fully staffed marketing department in-house, you may only need an

SEO firm. Conversely, if you're just starting out, a smaller business, or have limited in-house resources, a full-service firm, one-stop-shop is probably your best bet. Keep an eye out for firms that call themselves full service but are really niche!

- **Full Service.** Set up to handle a wide variety of client needs, full service firms are ideal for startups or businesses that have limited in-house resources. They're designed to take your marketing program through various stages, from initial strategy into branding and all the way through implementation. It's not uncommon for a business to stay with this type of firm for years and years.

- **Niche.** Niche firms are specialists in one or two marketing services. They can work with your internal team, other consultants, or provide single project-type work as needed. You may decide you need a niche firm to round out a campaign or to help you through business cycle needs, or as an additional and ongoing member of your marketing team. SEO and social media are niche-type firms.

Whatever type of firm you decide is necessary, you should always vet it for expertise and experience before signing a contract. This should be a common sense practice with any outside hire, but seems to be especially true in marketing, a field that is fraught with 'overnight professionals.' Adding marketing to an existing business's service list or a personal resume is not uncommon, and it's in your business's best interest to make sure the firm handling your work is an expert in that field.

As an outside consultant, your marketing firm should have one goal in your relationship: helping you achieve growth. You should feel that anyone you hire is a professionally invested part of your team and someone who will take the time to understand your business and marketing challenges before starting a project. If, for example, your consulting firm doesn't have an experienced marketer conduct exhaustive, business-specific research before developing your high level strategy, brand, or campaign concept, its not helping your business and is probably a waste of money. After all, any marketing firm's existence relies on applying its consultants' collective expertise to business growth and awareness challenges. It should do the same with yours!

Typical marketing firms you'll encounter include:

Marketing Strategists

The highest level within the marketing world, **marketing strategists** can take any size business, at any stage, and develop a plan for achieving growth. Using the steps outlined in Chapters 2, 3, and 4, your strategist will evaluate your business in terms of brand, buyers, marketplace, and current program before making recommendations. Her work should always incorporate your business's unique goals and resources, otherwise the plan is of no use. These firms can create your program from scratch or audit an existing one, and are experts at writing marketing strategies and plans. They can also help you develop specific campaigns and programs based on your unique needs.

When hiring a marketing strategy firm, it's best to find a firm who will assign a consultant who is experienced, has successfully helmed business expansions or marketing departments in growing businesses, and has a vast breadth of marketing knowledge. Experience will help her guide your business away from trends and gimmicks and toward a strong marketing foundation that you can build upon. Deep knowledge and understanding of how the modern marketing world works will help her propose a marketing mix suitable for your buyers and budget. As we saw in Chapter 2, there are too many steps that must be taken in developing a successful program to cut corners, and you'll want your program in the hands of someone who knows,and has experienced, marketing inside and out.

Vetting your marketing strategist consultant is your responsibility, and common questions you should ask to assess her skill level, include:

• How many years has she worked as a marketer *only* (as opposed to as a graphic designer in a marketing department or print shop owner, for example)? What roles did she hold and at what level? Again, you'll want someone with strategic experience.

- Ask about her business growth experience, including examples, and knowledge about marketing programs. What size were these businesses and how much of a budget did she have to spend? Did she make the most of the budget?

- What growth achievements or accolades have her businesses earned, based on her marketing stewardship?

- If you're looking at multi-market, national, or international growth, ask about her experience marketing at that level. For example, a marketing firm that has only worked locally may not be your best choice for an international strategy.

- What types of marketing projects has she worked on in the past? Is she well-rounded and able to advise on traditional and digital projects equally?

Your marketing strategy, plan, program development, and audits are vital projects that will help your business stay on track and in front of your buyers. Make sure you have the right team member to help guide you through the process!

Branding

Branding firms are focused on developing and implementing your business's brand details, as outlined in Chapter 3. They can help you develop your brand style from scratch or help you through a re-branding effort. Branding firms walk a fine line between creative and data, drawing inspiration and information from each. Their goal is to create a unique and memorable identity that draws on as many senses as logic dictates, given your business's industry and offerings. They must also thoroughly and completely research and appreciate your targeted buyer and marketplace.

You'll want a consulting firm experienced in both developing a branding program from scratch and business-wide implementation. This is a task beyond most graphic design houses, who typically focus on a logo and color scheme rather than a brand as a business-wide marketing effort. Instead, developing a successful brand requires an expert in interpreting data and capitalizing on business strengths who can then translate that information into tangible, embraceable cues.

Vetting a branding firm that will help you create awareness in your buyers' minds is similar in process to finding a marketing strategy firm, with a similar consultant question list:

- How many years has she worked in brand development and implementation? At what level and in what capacity?

- How have her brands contributed to business growth? What size were these businesses?

- What areas of branding has she worked within? Does she have expertise in all or most of a brand identity's areas?

- Does she have experience with developing brand architecture (if it applies to your business)?

- What is her multi-market, national, or international branding experience?

Once you have answers to the above questions, take a look at your own goals and marketing strategy and see if the branding firm is a match.

Communications

Although **marketing communications** is usually offered through a full service, strategic, or branding firm, you may run across a stand alone, niche firm. This type of firm may stress its copywriting services or present a more umbrella-like service list that includes content and communications campaigns. Given today's focus on content, it wouldn't be a shock to come across a marketing communications firm labeled as a content firm.

Marketing communications firms are experts at messaging and storytelling, which ideally applies to both traditional and digital marketing efforts. This is great news for their clients, but can make sorting through their marketing to find the firm's true story more of a challenge. Not all marketing communications firms are experts in all marketing project types, with some specializing in one type of work, like web content, over another, like white papers. Request project examples that are of the same type as your proposed efforts to find a best match. If your plans include multi-market or international work, make sure you find a firm experienced in successfully communicating within different cultures.

Vetting a marketing communications firm, and your assigned communications professional specifically, should include questions such as:

- How many years has she worked in marketing communications and campaign content creation? At what level and in what capacity?

- How have her communications efforts contributed to business growth? What sizes were these businesses?

- What is her communication area(s) of expertise? Does she have expertise in more than one or is she better at certain project types?

- Can she provide examples of communications projects she created? Did she manage these projects or was she a team member?

- What is her multi-market, national, or international communication experience?

Public Relations

The decision to hire a **PR firm** should mean that most of your marketing program's infrastructure is already in place. If not, soliciting coverage from the press is a poor decision because your one shot at reaching journalists will be blown by a half-created website, incomplete branding, or rough messaging. Of course, if you do approach a PR firm without that infrastructure in place and they start a campaign, you'll know you hired the wrong firm! Any firm worth its money will first check that your marketing image is ready for the big leagues and, if not, will create a to-do list before sending out the first release. Good PR firms understand the importance of marketing and will work with your marketing team to ensure a unified effort.

This is why one of the qualifiers in your hunt for a PR firm is its approach to marketing. If the firm only pushes press releases out to the media, it's not a true PR firm, but instead what is known as a **media relations firm**. These firms are more like distribution centers than true strategic partners. A true PR firm will bring up integrating your PR within your existing marketing program and will ask about your growth goals, overall marketing strategy, and available resources. It will also give you a long-term PR strategy without promising overnight rewards it can't deliver.

Vetting a PR firm should include firm-related questions as well as those directed to your assigned PR professional:

- What is her PR approach? What is the timeline and strategy she'd take with businesses like yours?

- How many years has she worked in public relations only? At what level and in what capacity?

- Does the firm, and more important, your consultant have strong media connections? With which media? If your business is more likely to seek print-based coverage, you won't want a firm that specializes in television, for example. Conversely, you won't want to hire a local agency that can only secure newspaper coverage in a small paper if you're trying to make a national splash.

- Has she achieved significant news coverage from her PR efforts? Is she able to demonstrate this over many clients or only a handful?

- What is her cross-platform PR experience? How about multi-market, national, or international PR?

Researchers

Considering the importance placed on **marketing research** and its results within your marketing program, it's no surprise that finding the right firm carries significant importance. Hopefully you've hired a strategic marketing firm that has research resources at its disposal, negating your need to hire a firm separately. If not, or if you're looking for a firm to gather specific data for an established business, then you'll first need to determine what type of research you need and find a firm that specializes in it.

As I'll discuss in Chapter 7, there are many facets to research, and not all research firms excel in, or offer, all research types. This is why you'll need to determine your research goal(s) before seeking a researcher type. There are some full-service research firms in the market; however, most are more specialized, meaning that your need may not fall under their service umbrellas. For example, a firm that's set up to conduct focus groups and has created its own research center may not be your first choice for analytics work. Or a firm that gathers, tracks, and reports market data may not offer secret shopper services. By narrowing your need down to a research type, you'll have a better chance of finding the right marketing partner.

Most firms fall into one of two high-level categories:

- **Field Research.** Firms that work with buyers in a personal setting, either one-on-one or in focus groups, are considered field researchers. They may collect data via in-person encounters, phone polls, surveys, field trials, focus groups, secret shop, etc. Field researchers collect data first-hand. These types of firms work well with response studies to products or services, customer service reports, or difficult to find data on your competition.

- **Analytics / Data Collection.** Analytics firms track, analyze, and report on data using research tools or business-specific algorithms. They're well suited to traffic and ROI studies, profiles, pre-market launches, and almost any parameter set required of your big data.

Your goal with any marketing researcher is to gain usable and actionable data, and her research approach and sample sizes used will influence your results. If, for example, hers is a local firm and her proposed sample size is in a geographically small area, she's not the best match with your USA-wide product launch. You want to find a researcher who can handle your need.

Vetting your marketing researcher always begins with your need and goals, and common questions you should ask to assess her skill level include:

- In what area of research is her expertise? How long and for whom has she conducted this research in the past?

- What is her research approach and how long does she estimate it will take to gather your data?

- What size were these businesses and how much of a budget did she have to spend?

- What deliverables does she offer and how does she present her findings?

- If you're looking at multi-market, national, or international growth, ask about her experience researching at that level.

- How will she work with your marketing team? If they have questions or different data needs, is she able to accommodate these requests?

Search Engine Optimization / Search Engine Management

SEO / SEM firms are dedicated to helping businesses achieve higher search engine rankings. Primarily focused on organic rankings, they may also work with PPC campaigns and search engine related advertising. Because an SEO program can take a little time to ramp up, these firms will typically work on a multi-month contract and incorporate a project mix of quality content and web visibility. The exact mix and techniques stressed will most likely change with each new search engine algorithm, but the goal of bringing your business to greater visibility and degree of credibility online should always remain.

SEO specific firms will work with you on optimizing your online presence, helping you distribute press releases, re-write content, register your business with online directories, and more. They should seek out any above-board and 'legal' opportunities that will drive your rankings higher. SEM firms will build upon that optimization and manage your SEO related activities and rankings over time, helping you maintain high organic results. You'll often find both efforts in the same firm.

Vetting an SEO / SEM firm is slightly different from marketing strategists and branding firms. For one thing, the field hasn't been around as long as other marketing professions, making questions about years in the role a little less relevant. Of course, be cautious with newly formed firms that haven't managed accounts over time. You'll want to put your trust in a consultant who has at least endured some of the changes search engines have implemented!

Things to check and ask an SEO / SEM firm include:

- Check the firm's own rankings by running searches on search engine firms, locally and in a wider geographic market.

- Run searches on the firm's name and evaluate the results by ranking.

- Ask how your consultant has handled search engine algorithm changes in the past and whether it had an impact on her clients' rankings

- Ask about her clients' sustainable results and how long it typically takes to see a change in ranking.

- If possible, ask about other clients' rankings. Run a few searches and check their results.

Make sure you understand what's involved in the firm's process before signing up (not the secret sauce, but to be as sure as possible that it uses above-board tactics). If your SEO specialist can't achieve top rankings with her own firm, how can she help you? Furthermore, if the firm can only maintain rankings for a couple of months, why would you enter into a six month or longer contract?

Social Media

Although different in specific work types, **social media firms** are similar to SEO / SEM firms in expected business longevity and your vetting process. Social media firms can help you identify the best social media channels that match with your buyer profile, develop an online social media presence, including incorporating your brand, create campaigns, and even post for you on a regular schedule.

Social media firms should be experts on the top social media channels while continuously keeping an eye on emerging channels and trends. They should understand what works best with each channel's audience, including the best posting times, styles, and frequency for your business to see ROI. They should also understand social media PPC and advertising options, and advise you on when and how to apply each. If a firm's business model is based on posting photos or inspiring quotes on Facebook, move along.

Vetting social media firms is similar to the SEO / SEM process. Legitimate firms are experts in social media and should be able to display a 'proof is in the pudding' presence on their own channels. Which is why you'll want to thoroughly investigate the firm's social media presence itself before reaching out.

Things to check and ask a social media firm include:

- Review the firm's social media pages. Evaluate them in terms of professional look and feel, the number of followers, and, most important, the quality of posts and social interactions. How long have the pages been in place? Are they active across multiple platforms? Are they posting a great deal with few followers? For example, a high number of tweets in Twitter coupled with low follower numbers suggests people aren't interested in what that firm is posting. A bad sign.

- Ask the consultant who will create campaigns and / or post for your business about her experience, years posting on clients behalf, and how she approaches social media with other clients. You'll want to confirm that a junior staff member won't be handling your account without your knowledge and permission.

- Ask about her clients' ROI and how she judges success with social media channels.

- If possible, look at a few client social media channels. Evaluate the quality of the posts and whether or not the consultant engages with followers and posts valuable content relevant to that business.

With a little sleuthing, you'll be able to find a social media firm that can help you with your own business's efforts. The trick is to look beyond a single channel page or high follower number and dig into the interactions themselves. For your business to have a chance at ROI, it has to be social in its social media efforts!

Printers

Print is not dead! Perhaps the twenty page business brochure is on the endangered list, but print's role within marketing is alive and kicking. Even

An offset printer working on a full color print project. Choosing your printer will depend on your project type, budget, and available time.

green or digitally-based businesses have printing needs in the form of packaging, user manuals, collateral, posters, or business cards. Odds are that you'll eventually find yourself needing a professional printer's help, and it's better to understand how they operate before your deadline hits.

There's an important difference between a professional printer and a copy shop, and your choice of if and when to use each will determine your projects' final look and feel. Professional printers generally offer superior equipment, a vast service and product lineup, and experienced, trained staff. The quality of your end product is directly dependent upon the quality of the printing equipment and its users, as are your printing options and ability to try something different. Unless you're running a few quick copies or a small project, you'll want to find a professional printer you can trust.

Professional printers will try to help clients out whenever possible, offering set-up suggestions, trend reports, and price break opportunities. It's well worth the time to develop a solid working relationship with your printer as they often help you make a deadline at the last minute, work through campaign challenges, or point you to an outside consultant, should you need it.

Digital vs. Traditional Press

The print industry underwent a radical change in recent decades with the introduction of digital printing presses. Heralded by marketers everywhere,

digital printing released businesses from the expensive and demanding traditional printing press and its color rules and run-based pricing. Digital printing allows for a more agile, personal printing program without losing quality. This was great news for marketing programs everywhere desperate for easy campaign-based printing options and a relief from budget woes.

What are the differences between digital printing and traditional printing? That answer can be broken down into three features that all relate to set-up time, labor management and turnaround time. Both printing options have a place in marketing and your choice will depend on your project:

- **Color**. Traditional printing presses, known as **offset printing**, require individual color printing plates, one for each CMYK color, and constant color management to ensure consistency and accuracy. This means that every time you add color in offset printing, you've added labor and cost to the pre-press setup and press management process.

  Not so with digital printers. Digital printing doesn't use plates at all, instead adopting a printing style similar (but of significantly higher quality and technology) to business printers. This eases the labor involved in color printing. With less labor, projects can be printed in full digital printing color at a more affordable price. Color control isn't sacrificed as modern digital presses have wide color scales and can match PMS colors.

- **Print Runs.** Unsurprisingly, production costs and speed are the driving factor in print run pricing. Short print runs in offset printing carry a higher price per piece due to the cost involved with setting up a file and managing the press. The larger the print run, the lower the per piece cost. Projects in the past had longer shelf lives because a larger print run was used to justify the project. Digital printing, on the other hand, employs a fast and nimble process that lowers the per unit price. On short to medium print runs, digital printing is the clear price and time winner, and its ease and pricing has reduced marketing waste and the need for storage rooms filled with dusty brochures.

- **Variable Data Printing.** Because digital printing is free from offset's static plates it can incorporate computer driven changes and personalization. Called **variable printing,** the process allows you to change words, data, and graphics on each printed piece. Incorporating personal variables such as names and graphics within the same print run has taken marketing to a new level. Variable data printing has found a home in the direct mail world, where you can, quite literally, address each recipient by name in your content. It will allow you to create custom content and tailor your project's individual piece imagery to match with buyers' past purchases or market data.

Offset printing is still commonly used for premium or large-run marketing projects as it often produces a sharper, more elegant image color control. Costs tip in its favor the larger the print number. You may find more paper stock and size options in offset printing, particularly if you want to print on heavily textured or thicker paper types.

Ultimately your project and budget will determine which type of printing you use. It's best to know your options ahead of time and listen to your printing partner on the best choices available. Many times they can offer advice on paper choices, print and binding styles, and delivery methods that will save you money.

Sending Files, Packaging

No matter which type of press you choose, your printed project will always start life as a file package. Unlike their digital counterparts, print marketing projects demand the highest resolution possible, typically 300 dpi or higher, and files in a printer-compatible format (see sidebar, *Need to Know: Graphic Terminology, Chapter 4*). Often this requires the assistance of a professional graphic designer, or at least professional design software.

Understanding what your printer needs ahead of time will help you meet project deadlines and stay on budget:

- **File Types.** Most professional printers will accept common graphic file types, such as .PDF, .EPS, .JPG, .PS, .PSD, .TIFF, .AI, or .ID. All attached or linked imagery must be in a high resolution format or you'll find yourself with pixelated graphics. Unless you're sending a flat image like a press-ready .PDF, you'll need to include all fonts and separate linked image files, including your logo, in your file package. Microsoft Word, PowerPoint, or other incompatible file types will require conversion into a .PDF before they can be printed.

- **Changes and Proofing.** Not all printers maintain a full design staff in-house and may be unable to help with design changes. Small edits can be made to original files sent to the printer; however, some may charge a small change fee. Changes can't be made to flat graphics like .JPGs or flattened .PDFs. The best practice is to thoroughly proof your files before sending. Keep important information at least 1/4" away from the file edges to prevent unfortunate trimming situations.

- **Color.** Projects that are destined for color offset printing may require additional color information. Specifying PMS color and mix details will help your printer hit your brand's color scheme and ensure that your final project looks as intended, no matter the press chosen. It's important to note that your project will look different professionally printed from what you saw on your computer screen or from on an office printer, which are not professionally calibrated on a daily basis. It may look darker or lighter than your in-office or proof version.

- **Embellishments.** In addition to file size and color specifications, your printer may ask if your want your project to bleed (print to the edge of the page), have a gloss or semi-gloss coating applied, bound in a certain way, or have special embellishments like die-cuts or foil additions. Other than coating and binding, any extra features will need to be built into your original file.

Printing Green

Printing can be environmentally friendly! Today's printers offer a vast array of green paper stock choices. In addition to recycled and post-consumer created papers, paper stock is available from sustainable forests. Intentionally planted and farmed using environmentally friendly farming guidelines, in some ways these papers are greener than recycled stock. Soy or vegetable-based inks are another environmentally friendly printing option.

If your project meets the requirements, you may choose to include the Forest Stewardship Council's (FSC), Rainforest Alliance, recycled, or other green printing logos.

Need To Know: Printing Terms

Artwork. All information that will be printed (graphics, content, photos).

Binding. The method by which multiple pages are collated and connected, usually on one side.

- **Coil Bind.** Uses a series of punched holes along one page edge, threaded by a plastic or metal wire.

- **Comb Bind.** Similar to coil, but instead of wire, uses a solid plastic comb with rounded teeth to connect the holes.

- **Perfect Bind.** Wraps a cover around inside pages and affixed along the spine with glue (paperback).

- **Saddle Stitch.** Uses wire staples on the center binding edge to hold the pages together.

Bleeds. An image area, usually 1/8" larger than your final project size, built into a design file that allows printers to seemingly print to the page's edge. The extra 1/8" is trimmed off, resulting in that print-to-edge look. Without bleeds, your file will have a paper-colored border around it.

Camera-Ready. Also called print-ready, a file ready to print with all colors, fonts, graphics, etc. prepared for the press.

CMYK. Abbreviation for the 4 process colors: cyan, magenta, yellow, and key (black).

Coated. Paper that has had an extra layer applied to create a reflective sheen and protective barrier. Can be applied pre- or post-printing. In pre-printing coating, the paper stock has been coated as part of its manufacturing process. Coated stock can enhance print quality and create a more substantial paper. In post-printing coating, a coating such as UV or varnish is applied. It is clear and can add a touch of gloss and image protection.

Die-Cut. A custom cut used to trim or cut out a design or trim style.

Dimensions. Your project's final, printed size.

Emboss. A raised image in paper caused by pressing the page over a shaped die.

Foil Emboss. Adding a metallic foil layer to an embossed image.

Fold. A crease formed in a piece of paper, creating separate panels. A once folded sheet of paper changes from two panels (front and back) to four panels, with the fold creating a panel divide.

Font package. The design and assembly information associated with your project's font. This information is housed in the font file.

Ganged. Printing two or more projects on the same sheet of paper, at the same time.

Gutter. The blank space, or channel, between two facing pages that is used to accommodate binding efforts.

Mock-Up. A printed and fully assembled version of your final project. Mock-ups are used to test your project before printing large numbers.

Print Ready. Same as camera-ready.

Proof. Similar to a mock-up, a proof is a printed example of the final project used to test it before a print run.

Score. A crease impressed into a piece of paper, allowing for precise and clean folding.

Separations. Used in offset printing where an image's color mix is broken out into the four colors, CMYK, and applied via four plates.

Spot Color. An isolated section of color in offset printing. Spot colors are applied using color plates. Spot color can be achieved via CMYK in digital printing.

Stock. A paper type, measured in pounds. A higher poundage number indicates a heavier or thicker paper. Stock can be coated or uncoated. Typical stock types include:

- **Cover Stock:** Thicker paper used in projects like book covers, posters, postcards, business cards, and heavier print projects. 50, 60, 65, 80, 90, 100, 130 lb.

- **Text:** Higher quality paper stock used in projects such as brochures and annual report pages. 60, 70, 80 lb.

- **Writing:** A lighter, quality stock used in letterhead and stationary projects, 20, 24 lb.

Trim. Cutting a page at design-dictated trim marks. Projects are often trimmed to your specified size, especially if bleeds are involved.

Designers & Creatives

Marketing would be a much more boring and colorless place without designers! They bring your logo and communications to visual life and make your websites a visually stimulating destination. Marketers depend on designers to realize campaign concepts, collateral, branding tools, websites, and much more. Not all designers handle the same types of projects, with most specializing in one form or another. Most designers fall under one of two high level classifications, print or digital.

Unless you come from a creative background yourself, you may find working with designers different from other consultant or supplier experiences. The nature of their work has led many design firms to adopt a more relaxed and fun-loving atmosphere, which is a sharp contrast to a typical business office. It's not unusual to find creative firms staffed by professionals who may think of themselves as artists first, business people second. Considering the types of work this field has generated over the years, it's not always an unfair self-assessment; however, it may clash with a "customer is always right" approach.

Here more than with any other consulting firm you may find yourself with an account executive or project manager consultant who acts as a go-between you and the rest of the design team. It's a structure that allows designers to focus on their work, not on client interactions, and ensures a consistent message and single point of contact. Many design firm staff models are based on a small mix of employees rounded out by contractors brought in as needed, and the firm may use your account executive as your permanent contact. In some situations, your project's designers may be fantastically talented in creative work and less so in client communications, making a meeting a less than ideal situation. Don't be offended by the single point of contact structure and, if you receive push back when you've asked to meet the team, there may be a reason that will have little impact on your project's success.

Typically, design firms, especially smaller firms, are not your best resource for strategic work, overall branding programs, and content creation because they seldom maintain a full marketing and research department on staff. Odds are you'll need to provide final content and campaign ideas to your design firm. Don't rely on your designer to write or edit your content.

Working With Designers

When working with designers, it's important to remember that design is subjective. Good designers will take the time to understand your business and brand before connecting, and the more information you share, the better armed they'll be when tackling your project. They aren't, however, data collectors, and few can and will conduct exhaustive market research before starting a project. Your best bet is to share what your marketing strategy has discovered in terms of your buyer profile, target market, and brand guidelines. Easier still is to work with a marketing firm that has design in-house or partners with a design firm.

Your project stands the best chance of success if you heed the following:

Design By Committee. Design approval by committee is almost always a bad idea. It's too easy to water down a project in trying to please everyone—someone has to be the ultimate decision maker for the project to move forward. Otherwise, you may find the process a struggle with your resulting project a poor imitation of its original potential after the committee picked it apart. Save yourself (and your designer) the headache and keep your committee small, if at all.

Provide Feedback. It's extremely important to deliver direct feedback rather than vague responses. Saying you don't like a design without saying what specifically bothers you won't help your designer make changes and perfect their work in the next round. Be direct ("the girl in that stock photo looks too old for my market. We need a 10-year-old, ideally in an active, outside setting," for example), but understand that design is a creative process that's not cut and dry.

Sending your designer feedback from multiple sources without first evaluating and prioritizing it yourself will have the same effect as a committee. Not every bit of feedback has value to your project. Opinions and feedback may stem from personal taste or simply to find fault, not whether the project is a positive match with your buying audience and brand. Consider the source and her motives before sending an email to your designer.

Dictating Design. There's little more frustrating to a designer than someone dictating a design's layout and elements. It's the surest way to have a designer phone in a design, rather than using her skills and talent to create something spectacular. You should share any necessary elements and your brand's style guide, but, unless you work in that field and see good and bad design every day, you'll want to let your designer earn her money.

My Project, Not My Files?

It's not uncommon for design firms, like photographers and videographers, to hold original work files, and charge, rightfully so, a substantial fee if you want them. Logos are an exception to this rule. The reason is that original files contain the career-earned technique and styles she used to create your project, and giving her secrets away is bad for business. Not only will this allow others to replicate her design work, but any inexpensive or junior designer could then make changes or updates at a fraction of the cost, sometimes passing the work off as her own. Instead, most design firms will send your printer, hosting service, or yourself a condensed or use-ready file.

You'll probably see industry standard language in your contract that says you'll be given usage or licensed rights to the work as contractually intended, but that the firm owns the original graphics and design files. That is, unless you purchase them, which will require another contract altogether. This treatment of original work is normal. Demanding original files without extra payment is like telling a caterer to bring food to your party and include the step-by-step recipe list and any ingredients necessary for you to replicate the meal later on, at no charge. It won't happen.

Print Design

Print Design Firms, as the name suggests, focus on printed marketing projects. Tapped for projects like collateral, postcards, annual reports, posters, trade show booths, packaging, menus, sales packages, and flyers, print designers are experts at generating designs that your buyers can feel and hold. They understand printing press nuances, page layout and file creation, and should have a working knowledge of direct mail layout requirements. A talented, professional design firm is a tremendous asset as their work will catch buyers walking by, assist in spreading your business's story, and, hopefully, encourage purchases.

Choosing the right print design firm will largely depend upon your project. You'll want to find one that's experienced in that project type, yet creative enough to produce unique, knockout design. The last thing you want is a discount firm that will deliver templated or recycled design. You also won't want to enlist a more artistic, poster designer for heavy layout work such as manuals or directories. Make sure you're working with a design firm that will assign an experienced professional to work on your project.

- **Print Design.** Print designers are the more artistic professionals in this field. They're the ones you'll tap for creative work and most design projects. They're the concept designers who will take a blank page and develop a logo, collateral piece, poster, etc. Some print designers can also create basic digital advertisements or social media graphics, which is useful when running a multi-channel campaign. Print designers can work on layout, of course, but copy-heavy projects are better suited for print production.

- **Print Production.** Production designers are masters of large text and copy layout. They work on manuals, directories, catalogs, magazines, newspapers, programs, etc. Projects with a lot of pages and words fall within a production designer's wheelhouse.

Make sure to investigate what will happen with your files after the project is over and what's involved with any changes or updates. You should expect to pay a fee for any changes in the future, including simple changes like a date or name.

Things to review and ask a print design firm include:

- How many years has the firm operated as a design firm? Younger design firms may lack experience working with clients or juggling multiple projects at once.

- What type of design projects are the firm's specialties? Make sure it's a match with your project.

- Review the firm's portfolio. Many design firms will have some portfolio pieces online, but it may not be complete or have every type of past project listed. You may ask to see additional pieces.

- Ask about your assigned designer's experience in your project type and review a portfolio, if available.

- Ask about the design firms client project results. Keep in mind that the projects may have been brought to them as part of a strategically formed, multi-channel campaign.

Web Designers & Developers

Marketing's strong push toward the digital world has led to an increase in **web-only firms**. These firms can create your business's online projects, bringing color and design to what could be boring pages. This is where your online storefront or event landing page can come to life, with as many bells and whistles added as your budget can afford.

Regardless of platform, your website's structure will have a foundation written in coded language.

Contrary to what most business people may think, a web designer and a web developer are not interchangeable skill sets, and it's important to know what you need before approaching a firm. Most web firms have the capabilities for each, but if it's a developer heavily firm with only basic design skills, your site will probably function well, but not wow anyone visually. Conversely, a design heavy firm can create the visual impact you need, but may not have the capabilities to develop more complex features like custom client portals or proprietary CMS.

- **Web Designer.** Web designers will work on your site's graphics, creating the visual look shown to the world. They will work with color, fonts, possibly custom graphics, and incorporate imagery.

- **Web Developer.** Web developers are the architects and construction workers in web work, and much of their effort is behind the scenes. They program, write code, and build your site's structure and functionality.

Be careful to screen your web firm for any add-on or ongoing pricing before you sign a contract. It's not uncommon for web firms to mark-up hosting and domain name purchases, and you won't want to fall victim to hidden fees or a firm that will hold your site financially hostage to monthly payments (as discussed in Chapter 4). You'll also want to investigate costs associated with future changes and if your chosen firm offers training to help you maintain your site yourself.

Funnily enough, not all web firms are current on the latest or trending technology. There are still web firms selling sites that aren't mobile-friendly, for example, and businesses pay them good money for outdated technology! Make sure the firm you hire offers at least what's common in the market, if not emerging technology.

Things to check and ask a web firm include:

- How many years has the firm been open as a web design firm? What is your designer's web-only experience? Older firms have experience but younger firms may be more apt to use the latest technology available.

- What type of web projects are the firm's specialties? Make sure it's a match with your project. For example, if you need an e-commerce site and the firm doesn't have e-commerce development resources available, it's not a match.

- Review the firm's portfolio and client web sites. Click through and test the sites on your laptop, phone, and tablets.

- Ask about your assigned designer within the firm's experience in your project type and review her portfolio, if available.

- Ask about the design firm's client results, based on its work. It's possible that the projects may have been brought to them as part of a strategically formed, multi-channel campaign. Ask!

Photographers & Videographers

Photography and video have long played an important role in business, but as the need for quality, relevant content continues to pressure businesses,

photographers and videographers have enjoyed an upswing in demand. Unlike other suppliers, there's a good chance that you'll work with an independent photographer or videographer rather than a full agency. This presents a different dynamic from working with a fully staffed firm, and you may find tasks such as scheduling and billing more of a challenge.

In some ways hiring the right photographer or videographer is easier than with other suppliers because the proof of skill is obvious. You'll either see a quality photo or compelling video or not. Concerns similar to setting up files properly for press or the ease of use programming in your website's back-end aren't as common. That's not to say that the process doesn't matter, as with the final cut of a video, but you'll experience fewer unknowns and can estimate quality by simply using your eyes.

Therefore, hiring a photographer or videographer begins with a review of her portfolio. As with any artistic profession, style and subject matter play a big role in final output. If, for example, you need a photographer for executive head shots, you probably don't want to hire a photojournalist who's used to capturing random scenes from life. You'll be better served by someone who understands how to pose a professional, has the proper backdrops and lighting, and presents a final file package useful in business. Similarly, if you're scheduling an emotionally charged commercial, you don't want a videographer who specializes in static testimonials or has limited equipment options.

While reviewing a portfolio, you'll want to see multiple quality examples of work similar in style with your intended project, not just a lucky one or two. Take a good look at the subject, lighting, and style used and assess that the professional's style and skills fit with your goals. You'll want someone who specializes in your project type:

Photographer. A professional who works with still, single frame photos useful in print and web projects. The "eye," or degree of talent your photographer possesses will be displayed on your final photo projects. Match the appropriate professional with your project's style and approach.

Photographer types include:

- **Studio.** Studio photographers maintain set-ups for staged photo shoots in their own locations. There are specialists within this category who provide head shots, catalog shots, product or food shots, etc.

- **On-Site.** On-site photographers bring the studio to you and are helpful for business shots such as buildings, interiors, process (as in manufacturing), board rooms, or just about anything you'll want to include in a collateral piece or annual report.

- **Event.** Event photographers roam your seminars, parties, exhibits, or other big events shooting crowd and group photos. They're used to approaching people and asking for a group photo, and should take enough photos to present a complete story of the event.

- **Photojournalist.** Not as concerned with making sure every attendee or executive is captured on film, or whether or not your president has spinach in her teeth, photojournalists are after stories told in a single frame. The more human or emotionally compelling the shots, the better. Photojournalists often work with media outlets.

Videographer. A professional who shoots in video or multi-frame film. Useful for business videos, how-to's, events, and anything that might be appropriate for YouTube, your choice in professional will depend upon your intended use. Videographer types include:

- **Events.** Similar to event photographers, these videographers will craft a story out of a series of event videos.

- **Testimonials And Interviews.** These videographers are perfect for single-camera, staged shoots where the subject(s) remain in one location per video. They can be used to shoot simple how-to videos.

- **Promo And Commercials.** Videographers with a marketing eye can make your product or service look amazing in film. They won't necessarily write the script, but can bring the concept to life. Promos and commercials may be shot in a studio or the field.

- **Documentarians.** Similar to photojournalists, these videographers want to tell a story and may pull from a variety of video sources. These sources could range from interviews to news reports in the final cut. A documentarian may be a good choice for a more involved how-to video.

Once you decide on a professional type, you'll want to craft a project brief that gives your photographer and videographer insight into your project's usage and goals. Some photographers and videographers may want to retain the copyright on your photos and videos. If you wish to own these rights, discuss the requirements and process by which they're transferred to your business. You'll need to discuss final deliverables and file types, and whether or not you'll have editing input and proofing rounds, especially on projects like business videos.

Other questions to ask potential photographers and videographers include:

- Within what area of photography and videography is your area of expertise?

- Do you have experience working with similar projects as mine? If so, can you provide me with examples?

- What are your deliverable files? What if I want negatives or raw footage (unedited)?

- What is your scheduling procedure? What is your realistic file turnaround timeline?

- Do you have all of the necessary equipment to shoot my project on hand? This is important with shoot variables, such as if the event hall is more darkly lit than expected.

- What is your payment structure? Is it by the job or will I have to cover extra hours and travel expenses?

- What is your availability to travel? What are the costs and scheduling requirements involved with travel? This may be a factor should you want to send her on location or to other markets.

- What editing options do you provide?

App, Animator, & Game Designers

Not surprisingly, hiring an app, animation, or game design or development firm isn't dissimilar from hiring other designers and developers. Before hiring, you'll need to understand your consultant's limitations in terms of software, platform, skill, and scope. You may find that the most talented designer or developer available is useless because she works on a platform not favored by your buyer profile. Depending on your project's scope and intended usage, your project may need story creators, writers, and other designers involved in its creation.

Much like web firms, your app and game projects will require both development and design components, and, ideally, UX influence. Apps and game projects require digital storytelling. Your project's outcome and usability is directly dependent on your chosen firm's depth of skills on all areas of the project, so make sure you evaluate the firm's expertise and personally review and use work examples. These projects can be quite expensive, which makes finding a professional firm that understands your needs, can stay on schedule and budget, and will provide a fully functional final product extremely important. The basic roles within these firms, include:

- **App Designer.** Similar to web designers in approach, the app designer is concerned with the visual side of your app and may play a part in the app's overall purpose and story flow. The app designer's approach is a combination of web design and UX, with design influencing usability and experience. Note, there are UX professionals who specialize in apps and games. Your budget will dictate whether you can include UX in your project.

- **App Developer.** The professional who builds a mobile phone or tablet app's structure, including programming it for different devices and platforms. Developers are focused on the app's usability and stability, not necessarily the visual look and feel. It's important to find a developer experienced in your end-use device's platform. If your developer is experienced in iOS, for example, you may receive an app that works well on iPhones and iPads, but not at all on Android devices.

- **Animator.** Animation covers a wide variety of professionals who excel at creating computer-generated or hand-drawn graphics used in videos. These professionals combine design and developer skills to create advertisements, how-to's, teasers, and much more. They can pull almost any subject into their videos, ranging from white board writing to your business's mascot, and use transitions, movement, and other animation techniques to create interest and tell the story.

- **Game Designer.** The game designer, on the other hand, is responsible for designing the visual concept and individual components. Backgrounds, icons, characters, game pieces, and much more originate with game designers. The game designer may influence the style of the game through design.

- **Game Developer.** The professional in charge of constructing a game. Game developers use the overall concept, individual graphics, commands, stages, and all other pieces related to the game to build out worlds, missions, levels, and more. The game developer is responsible for a game's stability and playability.

You may feel a freelancer is your best option for one of the above projects.

If you decide to work with a freelancer, make sure she's up to the job or has resources she can tap, as needed. As tempting as it may be, hiring a student or someone fresh out of school is usually not a wise decision. Junior professionals often lack practical experience and market understanding, as well as the project management skills required to handle big jobs on their own. They could end up costing you more money in lost time and personal involvement than if you had hired an experienced firm in the first place.

As with web firms, you'll want to make sure your choice uses the latest technology and styles, otherwise your expensive project may be outdated before it's released. Things to check and ask an app, animation, or game firm include:

- How many years has the firm been open as a firm?

- What type of projects are the firm's specialties? Make sure it's a match with your project.

- Within what software or device platform(s) is your assigned team member experienced?

- Review the firm's portfolio. Is its past work, style, and usability a fit with your goals?

- Ask about your assigned team's experience in your project type and use / play projects from their portfolios.

- Ask about the firm's client results, based on its work.

- Confirm how the project will be available to users. Will the firm set up a page in app stores, for example, or is that your business's responsibility?

Writers

Every once in a while your marketing projects may require hiring a **writer**. Writers, also known as copywriters, focus on generating written content. They often specialize in a writing project type or style, such as blogs or collateral, and are useful if you're generating projects peripherally (or completely unrelated) to your overall marketing efforts. Unless you're piecemealing a department together outside of a strategic firm, your marketing firm will use its own writers.

Not all writers are interchangeable, and it's important to find the right one for your project. I most frequently call upon creative business and journalist-type writers rather than technical writers who excel at projects like proposals or manuals. Typical writer types you'll encounter in marketing include:

- **Creative Writer (Marketing).** Different from fictional book authors, marketing's creative writers are masters of slogans, advertisements, persuasive copy, etc. They can 'spin' words and are often a part of brand development teams. Creative writers are useful in creating campaign components.

- **Web Content Writer.** These writers create web content, or web copy, specifically for your website pages and blogs. Social media posts are another possible project.

- **Business Writer.** Perfect for business boilerplate, management biographies, white papers, etc., business writers employ a more conservative, professional style from creative writers. You may use this writer to help with proposal bids.

- **Technical Writer.** Similar to business writers, these writers are often tasked with heavier, technical topics such as those found in training manuals. This type of writer is usually a part of a proposal team.

- **Journalist.** While not as commonly found in marketing, it may be helpful to hire a journalist to write articles, company announcements, and press releases.

Writers are used to being hired by project rather than hours worked. They're typically priced by number of words and, sometimes, writing style type. Hiring a writer is similar to hiring a photographer or videographer in that you can judge her skills entirely from what's in her portfolio and you should always review any pieces similar to your proposed project. Check that her style is a match with your brand's voice, and that she is an engaging writer.

When hiring a writer you should ask questions such as:

- How many years has she written business materials? In what capacity and for what end-use?

- How have her writing efforts contributed to business growth? What size were these businesses?

- What is her writing style and approach? Does she have expertise in one type of writing over another?

- Can she provide examples of writing projects she created on marketing's behalf? How did she work with the marketing team?

- What is her multi-marketing, national, or international communication experience?

Need To Know: Consultant & Supplier Titles

There are any number of titles available within the marketing world, each with its own spin or niche skill set, however, the following are the typical types of titles you'll encounter.

Marketing

Marketing Director. In some businesses, the Marketing Director may be the top level marketing professional who runs the department, manages the team, makes strategic decisions, and reports directly to a president or senior leader. Larger businesses may replace the title with or add a management level to the director that involves a Vice President, Principal, and / or Chief Marketing Officer (CMO), denoting increasing responsibility and power.

Marketing Manager. A mid-level person who manages day to day activities and may project manage. Generally doesn't come up with campaign concepts or strategies, but is the one who executes plans and will keep your projects and department moving along.

Marketing Coordinator. The junior member of a marketing team, this role typically involves assistant work, schedule maintenance, and routine activities. Marketing coordinators rarely manage marketing projects or work on strategic efforts.

Copywriter. As the name suggests, this person is a writer, often specializing in a format type (marketing materials, blogs, web content). This title is often preceded by a rank, such as senior or junior.

Marketing Researcher. The data-focused member of a marketing team. This person gathers and analyzes data and presents data-driven results and reports.

PR Executive. A PR project manager and client account contact responsible for maintaining a project's schedule and achieving client goals. Works with the media and may act as its main point of contact.

Media Buyer. A professional responsible for securing advertising spots, proposing advertising times, and negotiating best placement rates.

Design

Creative Director. The top level creative professional who manages the department and interfaces directly with senior management. This person will develop concepts and approve final designs and client presentations. Often the most visible creative professional who interacts with clients.

Art Director. Like a marketing manager, this person keeps a creative department and its projects running. This person will work directly with designers, helping or outright managing day to day projects, and will interface with the Creative Director.

Print Designer. A graphic designer who specializes in print-based design such as postcards, brochures, posters, and trade show booths. Generally this type of designer does little to no web-based work and isn't a good choice as a web designer, but may be called upon to adapt a print ad to static web specifications.

Production Designer. A form of print designer, production designers excel in large text layout and pre-press work. You would use this type of designer for heavy text projects like directories, catalogs, and guides.

Web Designer. A graphic designer specializing in online work, including websites and digital advertisements. This person may know how to write a little code, but generally doesn't build a website and its components from scratch using programming skills.

Web Developer. The one responsible for the programming side of your website. This person loves to code and construct websites and their components, but is typically not a design or aesthetics expert.

UX Designer. A designer focused on the overall usability of a website, particularly in terms of flow and layout structure. Related titles include Information Architect, User Interface Designer, and Wireframes Designer.

App Designer. A designer who is concerned with the visual side of an app and its graphical components.

App Developer. A developer who specializes in the structure and usability of an app. The app's builder.

Animator. Animators are a designer / developer hybrid who bring computer-generated or hand-drawn graphics to life via video.

Other

Account Executive. A project manager and sales executive focused on client interactions who may act as a liaison between a client and project team. This is usually your primary contact within a firm.

Project Manager. The person responsible for managing a project's moving parts and keeping a project on schedule, often used as a secondary title, such as in the case of "Sr. Web Developer and Project Manager."

Business Development. A sales-focused person who takes on additional tasks which often include staffing trade show booths, networking functions, or public relations events.

Bad Client Actions

Your ongoing success with outside consultants and suppliers will depend on both of you maintaining a positive professional relationship. Follow the golden rule: do unto others as you'd like done unto you. This doesn't sound too difficult if you follow what's outlined in this chapter; however, there are select client actions previously unmentioned that can negatively impact your relationship and, in turn, your project or ability to work with that consultant or supplier in the future. People will endure quite a bit for a good paying client, but, if your actions cause their business to lose money, your account is not worth keeping.

Radio Silence, Project Killer

Generally speaking, consultants and suppliers won't reach out and ask a question unless it's important. This is a good practice! Communication may be simply confirming a detail before moving to the next stage or could be sharing a major road block that has stopped the project entirely. Regardless of 'why,' radio silence is always the wrong response. Your communication doesn't have to be long, but should answer the question(s) at hand in a professional manner if your project is to stay on track. If you don't respond at all, don't be surprised if your project stalls out or isn't what you expected.

Withholding Information

Outside consultants and suppliers are just that, outside. Without the advantage of combing through all of your files, historic data, and offices, there's no way she can possess a complete picture of your business without your input. Past projects, legal or industry requirements, budget limitations, important deadlines, and more should be supplied by you. Transparency and business data will help your consultant and suppliers provide you with the best possible project work.

Vague Or Off-Topic Responses

Vague or uncommitted answers are almost as bad as radio silence. If your consultant or supplier asks for specific information such as, "will this image work with your brand's guidelines?" and your sole response is "maybe. . . ," he or she is no better educated on your personal preference than before the question was asked. Answering a communication with your own completely different question while ignoring the original request is just as bad. For example, answering the above question with, "can we look at starting radio ads next month?" is far from helpful.

Engaged clients take the time to clearly answer questions as they're presented. If nothing else, a response such as, "let me spend some time reviewing this before sending you my answer. You'll hear from me by noon tomorrow," ensures that everyone is on the same page and will dramatically cut down revisions and project issues.

Smothering With Communication

Conversely, too much client communication can be a bad practice. This doesn't mean a client should never reach out and ask questions or provide details; rather, clients who abuse the line of communication can be just as detrimental to the project's process. Asking if a project is finished well before the agreed-upon deadline or sending answers or information over too many communications (when they could have been easily combined) is annoying. Sharing too much personal information or treating your consultant or supplier as a coach or therapist is creepy. Random, late night emails with "I had a thought" only to change your mind again the next morning is unprofessional.

Don't make your consultant or supplier uncomfortable and force a change in your relationship. Keep your communications professional and within reason.

Meeting Deadlines

Consultants and suppliers work best with an agreed upon deadline, which is why the "when will you need this?" question is asked early on. Teams will be put into place, work performed, and deliverables sent all according to when you say you'll need your project completed. Do your best to plan ahead and contact your consultant and supplier well before your deadline. This will give her time to secure her best resources for the work and your project's spot on her schedule. Accelerated deadlines may be a challenge, but not always impossible, and most consultants and suppliers will do their best to speed the process, sometimes tacking on a rush fee which may be used to cover late hours or overtime, additional team members, or the chaos associated with re-working a schedule.

In marketing, deadlines apply to more than a project's deliverable. You'll expect your project by the agreed upon deadline, and your consultants or suppliers will expect you to provide all requested project information and payments on time, as required by the contract's terms. While not sending in requested information will result in delays on your project's work, hurting your business, not sending payments can hurt independent contractors or smaller firms that have forecasted the income and have to pay employees or suppliers who contributed to your project. It's a good practice to only sign a contract when you're ready to meet its terms!

Excessive Meetings

Just as time affects your own marketing program's budget, time and, more specifically, meeting time, affects your consultant and supplier's project budget. Your contact will be happy to speak with you about your project needs before writing a proposal, and more than likely (especially with consultants) will communicate with you when your project kicks off, if any issues crop up, and once it's complete, but more than that may not be necessary to satisfy your need and create a successful project.

A good relationship is important and involves mutual respect for each others' time. While it may sound counter-intuitive to customer service or sales, it's not always possible for your consultants or suppliers to meet with you in person or fit in a last-minute conference call. Most consultants and suppliers will do their best to make sure you're comfortable with the project at hand and answer your questions as quickly and richly as possible, but abusing your power as the client by requesting too many meetings or regularly demanding last minute attention can annoy even the most customer service-focused.

Along the same lines, requesting a "quick cup of coffee" or "meet at the office" from a consultant or supplier early on when you're only in the tire kicking stage, can unnecessarily mislead her into expecting an immediate business opportunity. Asking your contact to meet with you to "pick her brain" or requesting a review of a marketing project without paying for the knowledge is downright rude. Be up front in these situations and let your contact know that you're gathering information, but you don't want to take up too much of her time. More likely than not, your contact will offer a thirty minute phone call that will more than satisfy your questions enough to take you through to the next level.

Between travel time and discussions that inevitably go long, in-person meetings may not be economically feasible, or necessary, for all of your marketing projects. Our world is becoming more digital and accessible, through video chat, email, and texting, and consultants and suppliers use these tools to quickly and more thoroughly satisfy and manage ever-expanding geographic client bases. Unless your consultant or supplier contact is a full-time sales person, your project work location-dependent, or you've requested a large-scale, higher dollar project requiring business-wide work, you may find in-person meetings aren't all that important to your project's success.

Excessive Or Vague Revision Requests

Proofing and revisions are a part of any marketing project; however, some clients can fall into a revision trap where changes are made, and re-made, at every stage. Off-brand and outright errors in projects will need to be corrected, of course, but consider that if you've communicated all information requested clearly and directly and worked diligently with your consultant and supplier, your project should never have been off-brand in the first place.

From your consultants' and suppliers' point of view, clients who fall into the revision trap are problematic. Why? Because those who fall into this trap take their revisions beyond standard project corrections and improvement suggestions and into the world of nitpicking perfectionism. This can manifest itself in multiple rounds of revisions, revisions with vague instructions, trickling corrections in versus ganging them together, or making changes only to change them back later on. For a consultant or supplier, this is a sign that fear has taken over and you are reluctant to let the project go live.

You may be thinking that if it's your project and you're paying your consultants and suppliers for their work, then it's your right to make changes. This is true—to a point. Most consultants and suppliers are happy to work with you and make your project the best it can be . . . Until it costs them money or negatively affects your project. Unless you're paying your consultant or supplier by the hour (in which case you will have to pay for all time taken to make your changes), your project's contract price will have a stated amount of revision and proofing time / rounds built in. Excessive revisions that go beyond that time eat into your consultant or supplier's profit margin and eventually whittle it down to the point where she is losing money on your project.

How can this happen? Remember that even the simplest revisions take time, and compounded, this becomes a lot of time. Time must be taken to open a file (the larger the project, the bigger the file), make a change, and execute and send a new proof or prototype. If it's a change in concept or design, creative time must be factored in. Recorded projects may require bringing in talent and re-recording or shooting the project. Websites may require additional coding or back-end work just to move a component.

The point is that, yes, you have every right to request changes to achieve a best-possible project, but no, that doesn't entitle you to nitpick and monopolize your consultant or suppliers' time by ordering revision after revision beyond the scope of work (again, unless there has been an egregious error). Be clear and purposeful with your instructions, and combine as many changes into each round as possible. If your changes are due to a redirect in your own vision, offer to compensate for the additional time taken.

Changing Deadlines Or Terms

Along the same vein as excessive revisions, requested changes in deadlines or scope can cause issues and almost always costs one or both sides money. Situations that call for a change in deadline or project scope do happen, of course, but these types of changes should be avoided once a project is underway. Once your project has started, your consultant or supplier will have engaged her team, locked her calendar, ordered supplies, and put work hours toward the project itself.

Before reaching out to your consultant or supplier with a deadline or terms change, first stop and ask if the change is really necessary or a "it would be nice" situation. If it's really necessary, by all means reach out, but be forewarned that your changes may cause project delays or possible financial penalties. Outright cancellations often result in financial penalties, as most consultants and suppliers have terms in place to protect them against cancelled projects.

Asking For Free Work

Most consultants and suppliers are happy to hear from past clients, particularly if the relationship was positive throughout the project. They're also likely to answer any questions or offer basic advice, maybe re-send a file, even if their work with the client ended some time before. In these situations, consultants and suppliers view these helpful moments as value-added goodwill, and many hope it will help turn the client into a brand advocate, leading to more work and referrals.

This happy world can quickly turn awkward when the requests move past a quick question and into the 'free work' category. Asking a consultant or supplier to spend any significant time on your business without being paid can put her in a dicey situation, especially if you need her help right away. Your consultant or supplier will have to balance maintaining a good relationship with the loss of revenue or scheduling conflicts your request may demand or other clients your request may impact. How would you feel if your past buyers walked into your business and requested free products or services? You'd feel awkward and frustrated, wouldn't you? Then why would you expect your consultant or supplier to feel differently?

It happens that even the most innocent of requests can end up taking an hour or two, sometimes longer, which could, or, more likely, should have been spent on another project.

Projects your consultant or supplier worked on before are not immune to the free work taboo. Yes, you're entitled to help if there's an error or issue with your project caused by the consultant or supplier (and not you or your employees) shortly after delivery. If, on the other hand, your consultant or supplier has fulfilled the project's contract requirements, delivered a fully functioning and viable project, and time has passed since you last worked together, you're most likely outside of the project's grace period and requesting free work.

This shouldn't dissuade you from reaching out. The best course of action in this situation is to be respectful of your consultant or supplier's time and ask if she can help you, within what time frame, and at what rate. If you haven't asked for free work before and the request is simple, more likely than not there won't be a charge and she'll work you in as quickly as possible. Should she come back with a cost, don't take it personally!

7. I Think I Need Marketing Research?

In each chapter of this book I've stressed the importance of conducting research before creating or implementing marketing as this is the only way to ensure a completely custom program. Effective results can only be achieved through custom efforts, making research one of the most critical components in your entire program!

So what is **marketing research**? It takes many forms that all provide information about your buyers, marketplace, business offerings, competitors, or economic trends. It's the inside scoop on what's going on in your market and how buyers feel about your products and services. Through marketing research, you'll be able to mold your program, create profiles, and accurately understand your business's performance.

Your starting point will be choosing the type of research you'll need at what time. Not all research applies to each type of need, and knowing when and how to use your results is important. Marketing research is broken into:

- **Quantitative.** Quantitative research deals in measurable numbers. Populations numbers, age ranges, ROI, etc. are all quantitative.

- **Qualitative.** Qualitative research, on the other hand, deals with more subjective information. What product do you like better? Rank the quality of my service. What color is best, etc. are all qualitative research questions.

The value of marketing research comes from the accuracy and reliability of the data and the size of the sample. Generally speaking, data compiled by an independent source, in a neutral setting, from a large sample size is much more accurate than information pulled by a special interest group polling its members on an invested topic.

When developing a marketing research study, it's also important to understand the difference between:

- **Consumer Research.** Consumer or buyer-based research focuses on behaviors that lead to brand interaction and purchases. This type of research will study buyer motives and preferences that influence their purchase decisions.

- **Business To Business Research.** Similar to consumer research, business to business research explores the often more complex world of business to business marketing. This type of research may include business-related data such as financials or business histories, and is often used to influence business decisions.

Marketing research is further broken out into:

- **Exploratory Research.** This is research conducted before a clear objective has been defined. Its purpose is to help you narrow down your search and refine your problem. Exploratory research will help you choose the best methodology that will you satisfy your questions.

- **Descriptive Research.** Descriptive research is a "5 W's and an H" facts approach to collecting data and is useful in buyer and market profiling. It doesn't factor in motives or emotions; rather, it's solely interested in focusing your question and identifying clean parameters in your research. For example, "who are my businesses buyers and how do they use my products?"

- **Causal Research.** Known as "if / then" studies, causal research explores cause and effect relationships within marketing questions. For instance, "what will happen to my sales if my business re-brands this year?"

Research Steps

All research methodology options follow the same fundamental steps and principals. It's important to remain neutral and scientific while researching. Slanted or leading research will not help your business.

- **Define Your Need.** Research is always conducted to satisfy an informational need; therefore, the first step is identifying and clearly defining that need. Are you looking for numerical data to create a buyer profile? Behavioral based data before opening a location in a new market? The more clearly defined your need, the easier you'll find the research process.

- **Match The Research Type.** What methodology is best suited to resolving your need? Not all research methodology will yield the same results. Choose the right type.

- **Create A Source List.** Who or what sources can best provide the data identified by your need? Do you need information from your buyers or will a data resource suffice?

- **Determine Your Research Limitations.** Pulling data from every person or business in the world in an impossible task, which means that you'll need to define a realistic data parameter and corresponding sample size.

- **Write Your Data Collection Questions.** Your research will rely on a series of answers to your need's question(s). External research, especially in the case of surveys, focus groups, and polls, is constructed from a series of defined questions.

- **Gather Your Data.** This is the action stage of your research project during which you will actively collect data using your chosen research methodology.

- **Analyze And Interpret Your Data.** Once you've collected information, it's time to extrapolate useful data that answers your need's questions.

- **Report Your Findings.** Raw data and calculations are cumbersome and difficult to share with others. The last step in your research process is to take the collected data and create a summary report. These reports often include charts and graphs that visually display data.

Primary Data

Collected by you or your researcher, **primary data** is yours and yours alone. This is data that has been pulled by your chosen methodology, to address or answer your specific needs and questions. Because your business has instigated the research, you will shoulder all the costs and compilation responsibilities.

Surveys

A mainstay of marketing research, **surveys** are an easy way to reach out and ask buyers direct questions. Using either predefined or write-in answers. They can be crafted to yield results related to a specific product or service, marketplace, business image, or buyer behavior and are found in a variety of formats. Surveys can be anonymous, name optional, or forced name; however, you may find the best, most honest answers come from anonymous sources. Your response rates will vary depending on the type of survey method used, time of delivery, incentive, length, audience, etc.

Standard survey methods include:

- **Direct Mail.** Sending your survey via direct mail allows you to target audiences such as clients or past purchasers.

These surveys are frequently printed surveys sent with a pre-paid response envelope or emails sent via a service such as SurveyMonkey. Average response rates with direct mail can range between 8-20%.

- **In-Person.** Usually conducted in public settings, in-person surveys depend upon willing participants who will answer questions on the spot. Your audience can't be targeted and it's difficult to control and predict who will respond. This type of surveying can be expensive but yields very high response ratings, between 60-90%.

- **Online.** The most random of all survey types due to its unpredictable "whoever sees and clicks" sampling, online surveys can nonetheless gather valuable buyer opinions and anecdotal data. Response rates range between 5-15%.

- **Phone.** Do not call lists and overall reluctance to answer unfamiliar numbers has had an impact on phone surveys. With a warm phone list, these types of surveys can yield 45-60% response rates.

Regardless of what type you choose, your survey's success depends upon:

- Short, to the point questions

- A limited number of questions (no one wants to complete a long survey!)

- Answer options allowing respondents to select from a best to worst response range or write their own answers.

- Value to the recipient. Offering rewards like discount coupons or free gifts in exchange for a completed survey will greatly increase your response rates.

Never use leading or slanted survey questions. This type of questioning can turn off recipients or force them to choose an answer not in keeping with their own opinions. Your research has to remain neutral if you're to gain actionable results; therefore, balance must be sought in your question and response option design. Always include an option for comments.

Net Promoter Score

Surveys are useful in single research events or as ongoing marketing efforts. Continuously surveying your buyers, for example, can help you spot trends and identify buyer concerns before they become widespread. A popular buyer survey tool is the Net Promoter Score (NPS®). Different from customer satisfaction surveys, the NPS® gauges buyer loyalty based on one question "how likely is it that you would recommend (your business) to a friend or colleague?" Answers are given on a zero to 10 scale, 10 being the most loyal buyer, or a business 'promoter'. Zero is considered a 'detractor.' Scores are compiled by taking the percentage of respondents who answered a nine or 10 then subtracting the percentage of respondents who answered a zero through six. The resulting score indicates overall buyer loyalty on a -100 to +100 scale.

Polls

Unlike surveys, **polls** are used to gather quick answers to a single question. They typically use a set of pre-defined, multiple choice answers and may offer an "other" option where buyers could write in their own choice. Polls can be used in-person, online, or via the phone, and, due to their simple, one question format, often earn high response rates.

Focus Groups

A guided and in-person form of research, **focus groups** rely upon a small respondent control group queried in a neutral setting. Designed to solicit feedback on your products, services, or business, focus groups use a scripted question / answer format led by a moderator. Focus groups are often recorded and participant reactions to questions studied to gain better insight on anything from general brand awareness to favorite flavor choices.

Research can take many forms that may be responded to anonymously or in-person, such as with polling, shown here.

They're particularly useful in pre-product or service launch research before a business spends its marketing budget.

Great care must be taken by the researcher to remain neutral and avoid interjecting her own opinions into the questioning process. It's often helpful to have a one-sided mirror in a focus group room that will allow you to experience participant answers first-hand. The best, most balanced results often stem from multiple focus groups using fresh participants rather than a single group questioned again and again.

Interviews

One on one **interviews** take the focus group concept to a much more detailed, personal level. Using a researcher who guides a question and answer process, interviews explore a responder's answers in greater depth by allowing follow-up and exploratory questions. The result is a better understanding of a buyer's brand awareness, behavioral patterns, and emotional responses to your business and products or services. Usable interview data depends upon a neutral researcher who shies away from leading or loaded questions. For the data to mean anything, the answers have to be entirely the respondent's own.

Sample Testing

It's often advantageous to first test the waters on a new product or service before launching a full release. Known as **sample testing,** or simply testing, this form of research identifies targeted release sites, then carefully monitors results over a set period of time. Ideally, testing will show obvious buyer responses, good or bad, allowing the marketing your team to make necessary adjustments before a full launch date. Testing can be applied to anything from a new advertising campaign within an established market to a shift in retail layout to a new service titles. Anything can be tested, as long as the researchers can then track a change in sales, traffic, and profit.

Online Reviews

In Chapter 4, I mentioned the outward marketing advantages of establishing an **online review** presence, but didn't delve too deeply into its marketing research advantages. As with social media, online review sites provide buyers with a soapbox from which they can tout or trash your business, delivering first-hand buyer experience data. Many review sites include a quantitative ranking system, often from one to five stars, that can be aggregated by a time period or as an overall number.

Changes in your branding, customer service, locations, or offerings eventually find their way into reviews. Over time, these reviews present trackable data that demonstrate marketplace and buyer response patterns. Setting up review presences for different locations or separate products can help you compare business efforts with each other and review your approach within different marketplaces.

Not only will online reviews deliver first-hand reports on your business and its products or services, but they also provide reports on how you fare compared with your competition. Comparing your reviews against your competitors' can show the successes and failures of each business and help you improve your own marketing approach.

Observation

One of the most powerful research tools available is

simple observation. Through the use of video cameras, website heat map tracking, audio recordings, or any other personal observation tracking tool, researchers can follow buyer trends, reactions, and shopping patterns. Not only does observation offer first-hand records on buyer emotional responses to products, services, or even marketing itself, but it also tracks the amount of time spent with your marketing effort and involvement degree.

Observation can be invaluable at any stage, from start-up to re-branding. For example, a video camera set next to a display or within a research room can show you how your buyers touch and interact with your products (or marketing). This type of research will show any buyer challenges or frustrations, helping you identify flaws. It will also show complete disinterest or negative responses. It's a more invasive form research methodology that can yield amazing results.

Secondary Data

Not all of your marketing research activities will involve first-hand data collection. Often you can find **secondary data** that was researched and compiled for another purpose, but satisfies your data needs nicely. Secondary data can be pulled from a variety of sources, including government offices, special interest groups, media outlets, academic papers, or studies conducted by private businesses that, in turn, release the results to the public.

Secondary data can be a tremendous time and budget saver. While it won't often provide information on your own business's products or services, it can aid in developing market and buyer profiles, especially when you're looking to expand into new areas. Some secondary data, such as that provided by the government, is free to the public, while others may recoup costs via a pay per paper, membership purchase, or ongoing subscription service model. Your own research needs will determine what sources are a best match. Investigate and qualify the source before spending budget. Obtaining secondary data from the original research source is the best way to ensure data accuracy.

A perfect example of secondary data is the U.S. Census (www.census. gov), which provides detailed information on population make-up within a geographic parameter. Its information is free and will provide demographic details such as gender, age, race, income, housing prices, etc.

Marketing Analytics

Imagine that you have a process in place that would give you key marketing performance indicators such as effectiveness and ROI across your entire marketing program. Wouldn't that information be valuable to your marketing success? Having this information is not only achievable, but entirely possible with **marketing analytics**, a high level research butterfly net that pools results and data before creating metrics-based, analytical reports. Usually defined by a set time period, marketing analytics relies upon technology to create a marketing program snapshot that can draw information from your entire marketing mix and generate reports comparing your efforts over time, by campaign, or even against your competition.

Marketing analytics provides predictive and actionable reporting. Not only can it review and compare past efforts, but it can also monitor current efforts and help predict future outcomes. By pointing out weaknesses in your marketing program and identifying ROI efforts, marketing analytics acts as a data-driven litmus test for your strategy and marketing mix decisions.

Big Data

Heralded in board rooms worldwide, **big data** is one business tool that lives up to its hype. Much like content, big data has become a marketing and management level buzz phrase because it can be utilized by any business type, regardless of industry or size. It has found a home in the information-loving marketing world and appeals to marketing's need-answer-act process. Businesses all seem to have their own definitions of big data, making answering the question "what is big data" tough; however, most agree that it refers to information compiled internally and externally, collected and aggregated from a variety of traditional and digital sources that can then be accessibly analyzed and acted upon. Defined in terms of volume (amount of data), velocity (speed of gathering), and visualization (presentation of the data, such as charts), big data is massive in size, often measured in terabytes and petabytes.

Rather than treat numbers and data as independent bits of information, big data is concerned with the value of the information collected and how it interacts to answer a business question. Big data's advantage is in its application in decision-making efforts that, in turn, affect costs. Because it's question-based, big data is designed to pull from a variety of channels and generate a data-driven answer. **Data-driven marketing** is marketing that has been crafted around an original question's data-driven answers. In marketing, big data is classified into two categories:

- **Unstructured.** Derived from sources that don't follow a traditional, pre-determined data format. It's most commonly found in text-based data such as that found in social media posts.

- **Multi-Structured.** Big, cumbersome, and at times difficult to manage, multi-structured data is pulled from non-transactional buyer interactions such as tracking sensors, clickstreams, social media channels, web server logs, etc. The challenge with multi-structure data is in consolidating and using its vast results.

Success with big data stems from first asking a straight-forward question and determining if you have a tool(s) in place that tracks and subsequently answers it.

Big Software Tools

Answering questions with big data usually necessitates an integrated tool. If your business is large enough, you may choose to implement customized software designed by one of the larger brands in-house. While big data does require robust software to manage and digest its collections, not all big data resources are expensive or need to be integrated throughout your business. In-house software can have applications beyond your marketing department, and, depending on what type you choose, can integrate throughout your business as an overreaching management tool.

Fortunately, not all marketing's big data needs are met by expensive software. There are free and inexpensive tools that can help even the smallest businesses enter the big data game. If your budget is limited be prepared for a little work; these tools are usually focused, and it may take more than one to find your answer. One of the most common is **Google Analytics**, which can be added to your website as a visitor tracking tool, providing you with locations, entry links, time on site, and more.

New tools and data resources crop up every day as big data demands are made by more businesses, making it easier than ever to have your questions answered.

Customer Relationship Management

A **Customer Relationship Management (CRM)** system is a one-stop-shop housing your customer information. A mainstay of sales departments everywhere, CRMs collect customer-related data as basic as buyer contact information and past orders or as sophisticated as communication notes, complaints, and profiles. A CRM can help hone a mailing list or show conversion rates and profit by location at the click of a button.

More sophisticated software packages will provide you with more information options—at a cost. Popular CRM software includes Salesforce, ACT, and BuilderFusion. Not every CRM software package will work with every business or user type. It's best to try them out before making a purchase or you may find yourself with a CRM that's too cumbersome or complicated for your daily use, and if it's too complicated, you probably won't use it, leaving you both data and budget-poor.

Enterprise Resource Planning

Enterprise Resource Planning (ERP) is the CRM concept employed at a business-wide level. These business management software tools work with your business's organization as a whole, not solely your marketing and sales department. They do incorporate CRM and marketing, but their mission is to connect all business departments, from Human Resources to Accounting to Procurement, to a single core system. Invaluable in tracking resources and efforts, these software tools require a heavy investment in budget, infrastructure, and implementation time.

8. I Think I Can Evaluate My Results

Because many of your marketing efforts, particularly those distributed through the media or outside groups, aren't directly linked to a tracking system in your control, it can be difficult to evaluate results and calculate ROI. Without a direct connection between a marketing effort and a sale, you may find yourself wondering how you can gauge your marketing's effectiveness. It can be challenging at times, and this challenge compounds with multi-channel marketing programs that are traditionally run over a long time period and have many overlapping efforts.

Given the above, evaluations must cover both a set period of time as well as any individual marketing efforts with tracking capabilities, such as with your website. Time snapshots are especially valuable if you're running campaigns over multiple channels or testing out seasonal pushes. This will allow you to compare campaigns and determine what messages and styles had the greatest returns. More specifically, if a campaign is multi-channel or the tracked effort a piggyback on an ongoing message, you'll want to look at results over time and note spikes in buyer activity, especially as they might correspond with marketing efforts. Remember, generating interest through marketing is only the first step as you should always work toward upticks in profit and advancement toward your overall business goals.

Evaluating Results

Once you have results to track, you'll want to evaluate them by key indicators that can be turned into knowledge applied to future marketing efforts. This is nearly an impossible task without having some sort of capturing system in place that will help you identify patterns and emerging trends. Should buyer interaction in the form of leads or questions run through a separate department such as sales or customer service, make sure those departments are educated in your capturing system and overall data needs.

As I've discussed in earlier chapters, marketing is always interested in how and why buyers find a business, which is why you should ask every interested party:

- How did you find us?

- What need / interest led you to us (your business) today?

- Would you recommend us to a friend?

Given the brevity of some buyer interactions (retail), you may find asking more than the above difficult. Once asked, answers should be added to your capturing system. Through your capturing system, you should be able to pull indicators that feed into your buyer and market profiles and evaluate how your products and services are faring in the marketplace. You should be able to track this information from sales receipts or through initial buyer conversations. If neither is possible, such as in a busy retail situation, you can use the annoying but at times helpful zip code tracking system before allowing check-out. Phone numbers aren't as effective in today's cell phone world where buyers may keep a number from another market, skewing your results.

Trends you should continuously watch out for include:

- **Buyer Profile Indicators.** This is where you'll find out if your marketing message has properly targeted and, subsequently, lured in your targeted buyers. If not, and a pattern of different buyers emerges, it's worth re-visiting your buyer profile and identify why it's off. One or two different buyers can be considered outliers, but once the number starts to increase, you should investigate why. You may have discovered a new business opportunity or a messaging mismatch.

- **Market Profile Indicators.** Sadly, you may find that you have the perfect product or service but the wrong marketplace or location. They can show whether something has changed (or should) within your marketplace itself. Market indicators could show a wide variety of outside changes, ranging from roadway construction to shifts in neighborhood desirability that have impacted your business.

- **Marketing Successes.** Whenever possible, it is helpful to link a buyer directly to a marketing effort. The "how did you find us" question mentioned above should help you track what efforts bring in the most buyers. A quick note of caution, a buyer may tell you the most recent effort that brought her to your door and fail to mention the five other efforts that helped cement your brand in her mind. If she mentions something you can track, such as a mailing list, you will want to double-check how long she's been on the list and how much money you had to spend before finally making that sale.

Tracking

Determining your marketing program's effectiveness will require **tracking key measurements**. You may find some of your marketing efforts show you the most accurate results when tracked over time. You should review the following numbers continuously and by ROI.

Leads. The most obvious of all buyer metrics, you should know the lead numbers that answer:

- How many buyers responded to your individual marketing efforts and within what time range?

- What number of buyers responded to your campaign overall?

- What marketing efforts bring in the most leads? The most qualified leads? The best conversion rates (lead to purchase)?

- Did something change within a set period that affected the number of leads coming in the door?

- What are the conversion rates on leads to sales (the close rate)? How long did it take to convert a lead to a paying buyer?

Response Rates. Gathered from leads, traffic, clicks, and sales, you should know the response rates for every marketing effort in your program.

Website. As your most visible marketing effort, your website should be a major focus of your tracking efforts. Trends to follow include:

- **Visitors.** The number of unique and returning people on your website, the number of people overall, and all their locations.

- **Bounce Rate.** From what pages are visitors leaving your website? Did they visit only that page or can you track their path through your website?

- **Time Spent On Site.** How much time are visitors spending on your website?

- **Referring Sites.** How are visitors finding, then clicking to your website? Is it from an ad campaign, article, directory, or other source?

- **Click Through Rate (CTR) or Call to Action.** What, if any, call to action activities garner the most clicks?

Cost Per Response. Another way to evaluate ROI, cost per response and its cousin, cost per buyer, show how much you have to invest to get a response then make a sale.

Cost Per Response = (Marketing Costs By Market, Time Period, Etc.) Divided By (Number of Responders)

Sales And Profit. How has business changed in conjunction with your marketing efforts? If business hasn't picked up over time and you're executing all activities outlined in your marketing strategy, it may signal a need to perform more research and tweak the process. It could indicate missing research or a change in the marketplace itself.

Marketing should ultimately lead to higher sales and profit numbers, which is why it's imperative that this number is tracked alongside marketing efforts.

Returning Buyers vs. New Buyers. While it's always a positive marketing sign to see new buyers coming through your door, if the number of returning buyers is low (and yours is not a single purchase type business), there may be something broken in your process. It's far less expensive to keep a buyer than to lure in a new one, which is why low return buyer numbers could signal a need to change your buyer retention or buyer experience marketing efforts.

Leads

It's quite common for business owners to excitedly reference **leads** when asked if a marketing project works, but what's not as common is to hear about the quality and effort that went into obtaining that lead. Leads are nothing more than identified business opportunities, but, much like your wacky relative who solicits business investments from family members at reunions, not every opportunity is realistically profitable. For this reason, I prefer to track results in terms of profit and revenue rather than leads. The value of each lead is in its potential to make your business money, and if your marketing isn't bringing in profitable leads, something's off. This is why using a total lead count to gauge your marketing efforts' success isn't the wisest plan. After all, would you prefer to have a high number of leads that end up nowhere or only a handful that convert into sales?

While an in-depth review of leads and their usage can quickly shift into a sales discussion (which is another book altogether), there are a few things you should know about leads and how they impact marketing.

Types Of Leads

Not every lead is created equal, and knowing how to classify opportunities that arrive at your door is a critical driver in marketing success. Most companies use a version of the "good, better, best" classification system, and the easily employed temperature gauge classification is based on this concept:

Cold Leads. These are people who somehow landed on your list but have no, or little, interest in your brand. They may have signed up for a freebie, stopped by your trade show booth and dropped a card, secret shopped you for a competitor, or requested information, knowing that they can't afford your products or services, at least for the foreseeable future. However they found you, cold leads should never consume your marketing budget or redirect your efforts. While I wouldn't purge them from all of your mailing lists, you might drop your cold leads into their own list or category and only reach out with the most cost-effective efforts. Cold leads are a "no thanks" type of buyer.

Warm Leads. Unlike cold leads, warm leads offer a chance at making a sale. These are people who may be interested in your products or services, but need more information, time, or money before pulling the trigger. If you've crafted it properly, your brand message and content strategy should address many of these buyers' concerns, making converting these leads to hot an easier task. Warm leads are a "maybe, tell me more" type of buyer.

Hot Leads. Hot leads are people who have identified a need your products or services can satisfy, are receptive to your marketing, and may have already bought into your brand. These are people ready and able to make a purchase and only need someone to guide them through the sales closure process. Hot leads are a "this is exactly what I've been looking for. Where do I sign?" type of buyer.

Referral Leads. Referrals are typically the most valuable of all leads because someone the buyer trusts has already conducted a pre-qualification process and delivered a brand advocate pitch. They've literally been told, "this business can help you with your need. I recommend you contact them."

Leads As Indicators

Although they can't tell you everything about your business's reception within the marketplace, leads can nonetheless be a reliable marketing indicator. Not only can they provide first-hand information on who has responded to your efforts, but they can also help you track when and to what marketing efforts buyers have responded. Breaking this data down further can reveal what type of buyer (man vs. woman, location) responded to what type of marketing (online vs. traditional). With enough information, your business can create a historic, and actionable, knowledge base that will allow you to create highly custom marketing messages (women in this neighborhood who have purchased X product or service before). This is powerful stuff!

Your type of business will largely dictate the type of lead tracking tool you use. Retail businesses may opt for a **Point of Sale** software system that stores buyer information through a user account system or pulls information from payment details. Service based businesses may use a **Customer Relationship Management (CRM)** system (discussed in Chapter 7). More sophisticated software will provide you with more information options and come with a higher price tag.

Coupon Codes

Buyers may love **coupon codes** and special offers because of the discounts or add-on benefits, but marketers love them even more because they make tracking marketing activities easy. If you add a unique coupon or promo code to every marketing effort, you'll have a good idea of how many buyers saw, then acted, based on that individual effort. Coupon codes can be applied to traditional and digital marketing efforts, B2B and B2C, service and product businesses equally, making them a universally successful tracking trick. Over time you can use code results to demonstrate ROI and perfect your marketing messaging.

Coupon codes are not a fail-safe tracking tool. Some buyers forget to include coupon codes at the point of sale, and others share codes with friends, family, and, through online coupon collection sites, the Internet as a whole. You may have unrecorded sales that link back to a code or a code used by people who never saw your marketing at all.

Response Rates

Response rates, or the number of buyers who heeded your marketing efforts' calls to action and either contacted your business or clicked through an advertisement, are the most basic indicators of your program's success. Response rates aren't qualified data pieces that will tell you who purchased or the likelihood of a purchase; rather, they're straight-forward numbers that can be broken out by marketplace and buyer data, should you have that system in place. They can be calculated in every marketing effort that has a trackable connection, such as a coupon code, special offer, unique phone number, or link to a landing page or special online offer.

Calculating response rates is easy:

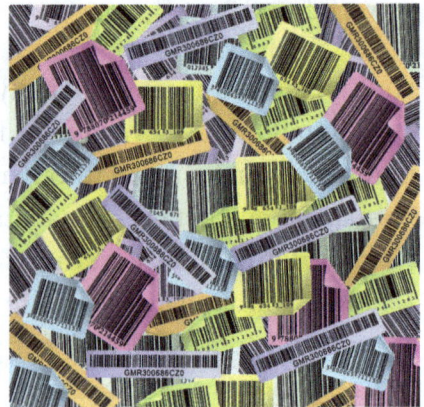

Response rates = (the Number of Respondents) Divided By (the Number of Marketing Pieces or Media Viewers) Multiplied By 100

So, if you send out 10,000 postcards and only received 400 responses, your response rate is 4%.

When calculating response rates in advertising, use the media's viewer / reader / listener numbers as your marketing number. Keep in mind that these response rates are traditionally low as not everyone will see your advertisement. Online advertisements and calls to action are calculated in clicks.

Clicks

Clicks, or the number of buyers who saw and activated your online or email marketing activities by clicking on a link or graphic, are another important indicator when evaluating marketing effort results. Click rates show the amount of online traffic your campaign or effort earned, and can directly tie this traffic to your website or landing page. Like response rates, clicks are a purely quantitative measurement, void of emotion-based data.

Click calculations are often referred to as **Click Through Rate (CTR)**, which is calculated by:

CTR = (the Number of People Who Clicked Through the Ad) Divided By (the Number of Impressions) Multiplied By 100.

So, if you have 187 people click through out of a potential 10,000 impressions, your CTR is 1.87%.

In email, the CTR is based on the total number of links clicked from an email or broken out to show a CTR for each link individually. In all digital marketing, the larger your CTR number, the more effective and successful your efforts.

Website Visitor Tracking

Tracking buyer behavior on your website is an ongoing process that can be reported and analyzed to reflect specified timeline activities, campaign efforts, or business changes. Using a variety of online tools, it's possible to have a complete picture of how and on what buyers focus as they navigate through your website.

Web Analytics. The overall data tracking process on your website's visitors is known as web analytics. Results-based visitors reporting metrics such as the number of unique vs. returning visitors and their page navigation, entry and exit points, time on site, and more fall under this evaluation tool. As I mentioned in Chapter 7, Google Analytics has become the standard for online tracking tools. There are other tools, but the free and powerful Google Analytics is the overwhelming favorite.

Heat Maps. You can view your website as your buyers have by tracking their movements via overlayed heat maps. Using a subscription service such as Crazy Egg, you'll be able to follow buyers' clicks and mouse movements throughout your website, giving first-hand data on component and overall effectiveness. Heat map tracking information will show you what information stands out and catches attention, and what is completely overlooked and by-passed.

Cookies. You can take web tracking further still through the use of web cookies and shopping cart / page tracking. These nuggets of web data activate when a buyer visits your website, particularly a product or service's page, and sends information to the buyer's web browser. The cookies then report back to you on buyer navigation and visit activity. In above-board uses, cookies remember buyer logins and preferences, making repeat visits easy. Below-board practices have prompted privacy regulation. Privacy laws have had an impact on cookie usage, as has the mobile market that doesn't use cookies at all.

9. I Think I Can Handle Success

This entire book has been leading you down the path toward your business achieving growth through marketing. By following the steps I've presented, you should have a marketing program that's accurately branded and finely tuned toward your buyers' needs. You'll have communication programs in place, metrics tracked, and a team of consultants and suppliers at your ready. In other words, you're prepared for business success. The question is, are you ready for it?

Surprising as it may seem, there are business owners who undertake major marketing efforts without any consideration of what will happen if they're successful. They may fund the effort, contribute to its process, then freeze right as the world is about to reward them with buyers aplenty. It's fitting to end this book with a discussion on what could happen if marketing is applied appropriately and your business is able to meet its goals. This isn't a pipe dream; your business really can grow and achieve results!

Considering all that can and does go wrong in business, a fear of success may not seem like a realistic problem. Certainly not when we consider the low number of businesses that actually achieve success. Betting odds are against most businesses achieving their goals. Maybe that's why some business owners are taken by surprise when marketing delivers buyers and growth their way? Perhaps.

If we look upon your business as if every marketing effort you try in the future will hit big, with buyers coming through the door faster than your credit card machines can process sales, what then? Have you taken steps to make sure your business's infrastructure is in place?

Something else to consider is whether or not you're mentally prepared for any changes that marketing may require. If marketing is focused on growth and attracting buyers, then any changes suggested in your strategy are only to your advantage, right? Then why do so many established businesses struggle with potential change when it's for their own good?

I'm a big advocate of smart business growth and building within as much as building out. By adopting an infrastructure-based, tiered goal approach, your business can enjoy the aforementioned best case scenario rather than becoming a victim of its own success. I work with my clients to set marketing goals in achievable steps, allowing them to meet demands and maintain sanity as they shore up weak spots within their business. We work on implementing marketing programs, including branding, throughout their businesses, allowing every employee to become a contributor to goals. This translates to many more shoulders that are prepped for the weight of a rush, ready to spring into action and lend a hand through any growing pains.

That's not to say big splashes don't have a place in business! Of course they do, and I've been involved in plenty. It's incredibly rewarding to be a part of an overnight success, and I wish more businesses were able to reap quick rewards. What I'm saying is that no marketing push, product release, grand opening, or press splash happens so quickly that a moment to consider "what if" can't be taken. Truthfully, it should have happened well before that moment, back when your marketing strategy was just coming to life.

While crafting your marketing strategy, spend at least a few moments jotting down what you'd do if everything worked out better than planned. It doesn't have to be an involved list or a section within your overall business plan (although kudos to you if it is). A basic list of who and what can be called upon to step in at a moment's notice, the lead and implementation time associated with software that should be put in place to process your orders, the customer service and new client on-boarding program that needs to be overhauled are all topics that should be addressed before you think of launching a major campaign. Because what will happen if the phone starts ringing uncontrollably?

If this book has accomplished nothing else, I hope it presented marketing as a real path toward growth, making that journey not only possible, but *probable*. Your business can grow, you can achieve your goals. Make sure you're ready for it!

Acknowledgements

Writing a book is a work of passion and dedication to an ideal. In my case, it involved more than myself, and without the following people, this book would not have become a reality:

My husband, Kiley, whose love and support helped me throughout this writing. His combined sympathetic ear and tough sounding board style guided and kept me going. He always believed in me and this book.

My mother, Kathleen, who has always, always been there when I've needed her. I'm so lucky to have her in my life.

My friend Karlene, who encouraged me to write this book and provided invaluable advice.

My friend, Laura, who kindly read through and checked sections in this book.

And my dog, Elliott, who stayed next to me through every typed word, edit, and re-write. You're a good boy.

Bibliography

Arthur, Lisa. "What Is Big Data?", *Forbes* August 15, 2013

Ciotti, Gregory. "The Psychology of Color in Marketing and Branding". *HelpScout.net blog.* August 6, 2013

Brummitt, James. "Business analytics: Big data now a tool for small business, Part 1" *CBiz.com blog,* March 19, 2015

Gillett, Rachel, "What Your Logo's Color Says About Your Company," *Fast Company,* March 31, 2014

"The Zero Moment of Truth Macro Study," Google and Shopper Sciences, April 2011.

Kerpen, Dave. "How Small Businesses Can Make Better Decisions with Big Data" *Inc.* April 7, 2015

Meyerson, Mitch. *Success Secrets of the Online Marketing Superstars.* Entrepreneur Press, 2015.

Simonson, Itamar and Emanuel Rosen, "What Marketers Misunderstand About Online Reviews" *Harvard Business Review,* January – February 2014 Issue.

Wheeler, Alina. *Designing Brand Identity.* New Jersey: John Wiley & Sons, Inc. 2013

About the Author

Bonnie Taylor loves growing businesses. It's been her passion for over 20 years in a career that's spanned local, national, and international campaigns and market launches. As the Chief Marketing Strategist and Owner of the Washington D.C. Metropolitan-based marketing firm, CCS Innovations®, LLC, she spends each day solving business puzzles and her clients' challenges, sourcing skills earned throughout her experience-rich marketing career.

It's her strategic, common sense approach mixed with a willingness to roll up her sleeves and get to work, no matter the obstacle, that has earned Bonnie a reputation as a business 'miracle worker'. Her skills have benefited businesses at all stages, from start-up to firmly established, in a wide range of industries.

Her diverse background has included marketing some of the world's biggest brands, such as Coca-Cola and Revlon, and countless smaller businesses. Bonnie has guided two companies from a single office without a marketing program to worldwide expansion in just a couple of years, earning *Inc.* 500 and *Business Journal* 'Fastest Growing Company' awards along the way.

Bonnie is an internationally published authority on marketing, branding, and corporate expansion. She is an avid equestrian and lives in Northern Virginia with her husband, Kiley.

You may contact Bonnie via her website IThinkINeed.com or email her at bonnie@ithinkineed.com.